T0016630

3 MINUTES
with
Jesus

3 MINUTES
with
Jesus

180 Devotions for Teen Girls

ELLIE ZUMBACH

BARBOUR
PUBLISHING

© 2023 by Barbour Publishing, Inc.

Print ISBN 978-1-63609-601-8

All rights reserved. No part of this publication may be reproduced or transmitted for commercial purposes, except for brief quotations in printed reviews, without written permission of the publisher. Reproduced text may not be used on the World Wide Web.

Churches and other noncommercial interests may reproduce portions of this book without the express written permission of Barbour Publishing, provided that the text does not exceed 500 words or 5 percent of the entire book, whichever is less, and that the text is not from material quoted from another publisher. When reproducing text from this book, include the following credit line: "From *3 Minutes with Jesus: 180 Devotions for Teen Girls*, published by Barbour Publishing, Inc. Used by permission."

Scripture quotations marked CSB have been taken from the Christian Standard Bible®, Copyright © 2017 by Holman Bible Publishers. Used by permission. Christian Standard Bible® and CSB® are federally registered trademarks of Holman Bible Publishers.

Scripture quotations marked NIV are taken from the HOLY BIBLE, NEW INTERNATIONAL VERSION®. NIV®. Copyright © 1973, 1978, 1984, 2011 by Biblica, Inc.™ Used by permission. All rights reserved worldwide.

Scripture quotations marked NLV are taken from the New Life Version copyright © 1969 and 2003 by Barbour Publishing, Inc., Uhrichsville, Ohio, 44683. All rights reserved.

Scripture quotations marked MSG are from *THE MESSAGE*. Copyright © by Eugene H. Peterson 1993, 1994, 1995, 1996, 2000, 2001, 2002. Used by permission of NavPress Publishing Group.

Published by Barbour Publishing, Inc., 1810 Barbour Drive, Uhrichsville, Ohio 44683, www.barbourbooks.com

Our mission is to inspire the world with the life-changing message of the Bible.

ECPA Member of the Evangelical Christian Publishers Association

Printed in China.

INTRODUCTION

Most days we're searching for a moment or two of inspiration, encouragement, and understanding—a fresh breath of air for the lungs and soul.

Here is a collection of moments from the true source of all inspiration and encouragement, the one who understands us greatly—Jesus. Within these pages you'll be guided through just-right-size readings that you can experience in as few as three minutes:

- Minute 1: Reflect on Jesus' life or words as written in God's Word
- Minute 2: Read real-life application and encouragement
- Minute 3: Pray

These devotions aren't meant to be a replacement for digging deep into the scriptures or for personal, in-depth quiet time. Instead, consider them a perfect jump-start to help you form a habit of spending time with Jesus every day. Or add them to the time you're already spending with Him. Jesus longs for us to have a relationship with Him as we navigate life, love, jobs, anxiety, our futures, and more. We were never meant to do it alone. Jesus is ready to make Himself known in your life.

"The people living in darkness have seen a great light; on those living in the land of the shadow of death a light has dawned."
MATTHEW 4:16 NIV

5

ONE OF HIS

He will stand and shepherd his flock in the
strength of the Lord. . . . And they will live
securely. . . . And he will be our peace.
MICAH 5:4–5 NIV

If you grew up in Sunday school, you've probably seen the many pictures of Jesus with His sheep. Some are cartoony and happy. Others are painted and serious. But what does Jesus as a shepherd really look like?

A shepherd's duty is to guard and protect his flock of sheep—every last one of them, no matter their age, size, or color. And because this flock knows their shepherd is taking care of them, they enjoy the most out of their worry-free and joyful sheep life.

Jesus wants to give the same to you as your shepherd. If you are one of His flock, He offers security and peace so you can live the fullest out of your amazing and beautiful human life. You just have to trust Him.

Dear Jesus, thank You for always being my shepherd.
I want You to be my sense of security and my access
to true peace. Help me trust You. Amen.

DO NOT BE AFRAID

*But the angel said to her, "Do not be afraid, Mary;
you have found favor with God. You will conceive and
give birth to a son, and you are to call him Jesus."*
LUKE 1:30–31 NIV

Mary, the mother of Jesus, didn't know how her family would react to the news of her pregnancy. Would they be angry? She had no idea if her soon-to-be husband, Joseph, would understand what had happened or if he'd even believe her. All she knew at that moment was that she was chosen by God to carry and have Jesus, the Son of God and Savior of the world. No big deal, right?

One of the first phrases ever associated with Jesus and His time on earth is "Do not be afraid." Out of all the news the angel shared with Mary, those were the words that mattered to her most. *Do not be afraid.* Because Jesus has the ability to replace fear with His presence.

---

*Dear Jesus, when I am scared of what I don't know,
please remind me that You are near and here for me.
I don't have to be afraid with You in my life.*

PERFECT REST

*"Come to Me, all of you who work and
have heavy loads. I will give you rest."*
MATTHEW 11:28 NLV

Sometimes there is nothing better than coming home to your nice cozy bed and slipping under the covers for a good night's rest, knowing that the morning is a brand-new day for a brand-new start. But, unfortunately, not all nights go so easy. Maybe you toss and turn about life's worries before a couple of hours of light shut-eye. Maybe you dread falling asleep because you don't want to wake up for one more day in this tough season.

We all have those kinds of nights. So God offered His children a solution. Jesus is the perfect place to go to for perfect rest. He asks us to lay down our burdens and worries, get rid of our heavy loads, and massage our tired shoulders. He wants us to find rest so we can live out the day as He designed us to. And the best time to ask Him to take your worries for your rest would be bedtime!

---

*Before I go to sleep, Jesus, I want to lay this
at Your feet: _____. Amen.*

NO PUNISHMENT

*"A Son will be born to her. You will give Him
the name Jesus because He will save His
people from the punishment of their sins."*
Matthew 1:21 nlv

Ever been called out for texting in class? Forced to move seats because you kept talking with your friend while the teacher was speaking? Have you ever been sent to the principal's office? Being punished for disobeying the rules at school can be not only embarrassing but scary! Will you be given a warning or a detention?

God tells us that there's a punishment for sins—those pesky things that take your eyes off all the good things in life and make you focus on the bad. That punishment is a total separation from Him.

So that's why God sent Jesus. Jesus saved His creation from the punishment of sin by taking it upon Himself on the cross. You don't have to worry about the punishment of being separated from God, because through Jesus you have been completely forgiven and redeemed.

Jesus, thank You so much for taking on my punishment. With this in mind, I will try to be the best version of me that I can be

FOCUSED

Jesus sat down and called the followers to Him. He said, "If anyone wants to be first, he must be last of all. He will be the one to care for all."
MARK 9:35 NLV

First place! Number one! Top of the pyramid! Being first makes you feel good because you're getting what you want, what you worked for, or what you feel you deserve. But that does have the possibility of starting some problems. Why? Because it is all about you.

That's not how Jesus looked at life. He kept His focus on those around Him, and He asked His disciples to do the same. This doesn't mean you shouldn't be proud of what you've done. This means that you're making sure you're looking out for, serving, and loving others when they really need it. Jesus shows you how to keep your focus on them by actively putting them before yourself.

Jesus, help me to stay focused on others so I can love them when they need it. Amen.

FRIEND

"I no longer call you servants, because a servant does not know his master's business. Instead, I have called you friends, for everything that I learned from my Father I have made known to you."

JOHN 15:15 NIV

Jesus isn't like a micromanaging boss. He is not in the back of your workplace, watching the cameras to make sure you don't act up. Jesus isn't like a discouraging coach, waiting for the moment you mess up to make you run lap after lap around the track.

No, Jesus wants you to know that He calls you friend. Because of everything He did on the cross, everything He shared while He was on earth, Jesus broke down that barrier that had once separated people from God. You can approach the throne of God as a friend.

Let that really sink in—you are Jesus' friend! One of His best friends. This means that you are never alone. You always have someone to talk to you and help you. What does being His friend mean to you? How will you treat Him as your friend?

Dear Jesus, thank You for calling me Your friend. Amen.

A SOLITARY PLACE

Very early in the morning, while it was still dark, Jesus got up, left the house and went off to a solitary place, where he prayed.
MARK 1:35 NIV

Ever woken up before the sun rose? In those early-morning hours, everything seems different: more still, more quiet, more. . .alone. But Jesus knew He wasn't alone. He got up early in the morning (maybe He'd already been up because of anxiety of what was to happen on the cross) and went off by Himself to pray.

Jesus showed that amazing prayer and communion with God can happen when you're alone and so anxious you have nowhere else to turn. When you're alone, you have no distractions. You have no expectations to meet about how you should sound or what you should say. You can just speak truthfully.

Jesus showed His followers that God wants to meet His children wherever they are at for real, life-changing conversations. Do you have a solitary place where you can go to speak with God?

Dear Jesus, thanks for giving me so many examples of different ways to pray. I want to find a place to be alone with You.

ACTED-OUT LOVE

"You are to love each other. You must love each other as I have loved you. If you love each other, all men will know you are My followers."
JOHN 13:34–35 NLV

When asked by the teachers of the law what's the most important commandment, Jesus said to love God and to love others (see Mark 12:29–32). He said it again to His disciples and told them that they *must* love each other as He loved them. He added a *must* the second time. Why was this important to Him?

Jesus was *perfect* at loving others. He lived out His love by helping others, teaching truth, and performing miracles. People knew who Jesus was because of His acted-out love. But after Jesus was gone from this world, Jesus knew that His love could only be shown through His followers that remained. He wanted to get them ready.

You have the chance and the ability to share Jesus with others by simply loving them. If you do that, you're doing what Jesus thought of as the most important commandment.

Jesus, help me to act out my love. Help me to love others the way You loved others. Amen.

WASHING FEET

*[Jesus] came to Simon Peter, who said to him,
"Lord, are you going to wash my feet?" Jesus
replied, "You do not realize now what I am
doing, but later you will understand."*

JOHN 13:6–7 NIV

Would you wash your best friend's feet? You might say yes, but what if you had to wash her feet after she had run barefoot for hours through mud and muck?

Jesus chose to wash His friends' feet—all twelve of them. And these were dudes who walked everywhere on dusty, desert roads, wearing only sandals. Because people's feet got so dirty, and it was a disgusting job, this task was given to the lowest servant of the household.

But Jesus did this task. When He finished, He said, "Now that I, your Lord and Teacher, have washed your feet, you also should wash one another's feet. I have set you an example" (John 13:14–15 NIV).

Jesus let His actions toward caring for others speak the loudest. You can do the same when you look around to see who needs some of your kindness.

Jesus, show me ways I can "wash someone's feet" today.

15

HALF-EMPTY OR HALF-FULL

And he subjected everything under his feet
and appointed him as head over everything
for the church, which is his body, the fullness
of the one who fills all things in every way.
EPHESIANS 1:22–23 CSB

You've probably heard the saying about seeing the glass half-full or half-empty. It tries to explain if you look at life with optimism or not. Do you still secretly hope that the glass will be filled to the top? Do you wish that good will always prevail and only amazing things will happen to those who deserve them?

Unfortunately, we live in a broken world, and what we want doesn't always happen. That's why we can't always rely on the way we look at the world to be happy. We have to look at it through Jesus' power. Jesus fills us with joy and peace, "all things in every way," no matter our circumstances.

When you're feeling empty because of what life has put in your glass, you can go to Jesus to refill it with His goodness.

Dear Jesus, I know You are the only one who
can truly fulfill me. Thank You.

WALK IN LOVE

*Walk in love, as Christ also loved
us and gave himself for us.*
EPHESIANS 5:2 CSB

You can start walking in love by reading about Jesus' life in the Gospels. But Paul also writes some examples that he gleaned out of his Savior's time on earth in Ephesians 4:25–5:5.

Always speak the truth to your friends. It's okay to be angry—even Jesus experienced anger (see John 2:13–17)—but don't let it rule over you. Don't steal. Always work hard at everything you do. Don't make fun of people; encourage others. Don't use sex to hurt others. Give thanks to God and to others. Share with those in need.

This long list can really be summed up in this verse: "Be kind and compassionate to one another, forgiving one another, just as God also forgave you in Christ" (Ephesians 4:32 CSB).

Jesus was the kindest and most compassionate person. He knew how to love everyone the right way. Though we may stumble in our walk in loving others, Jesus is there to help us.

---

*Jesus, I may stumble in my walk in loving others.
Thank You for being there every time.*

17

BASIS OF LOVE

For this reason, although I have great boldness
in Christ to command you to do what is right,
I appeal to you, instead, on the basis of love.
PHILEMON 8–9 CSB

One of the hardest things in life is when a friendship ends. Sometimes a friendship ends because of time, because of simply growing up and growing apart. No hard feelings. But sometimes friendships end because of hurt and broken promises. You may feel like it will never be repaired.

The book of Philemon is an example of how to seek reconciliation with another person Christ's way. No demands. No angry comments. No I'm-right-and-you're-wrongs. Paul asked Philemon to view a returning runaway slave, Onesimus, as a brother in Christ, not his property. He asked Philemon to see Onesimus with love, and make his decision toward their relationship with love—just as Jesus did with all His relationships.

Jesus asks us to do the same with our broken relationships today. Whether you are returning to a situation you left or you're the one needing to forgive, start where Jesus did—with love.

Jesus, this situation is hard. Help me to still
choose love in this hurt and brokenness.

GIVE YOU EVERYTHING!

"Don't be afraid of missing out. You're my dearest friends! The Father wants to give you the very kingdom itself."
LUKE 12:32 MSG

Ever been left out? It really stinks not to be invited to that party or not to get a gift when everyone else got one. Even though they may not mean to, people can be forgetful. And when things like that happen, *hurt* happens.

That's not the way with Jesus. He never forgets anyone and never leaves anyone out. His gift of eternal life is for everyone to receive. No one is left out, including you. He wants you to take the chance to experience and gain everything He has planned for your beautiful life on earth and after.

You're entirely His, and He claims you as His own. You won't be forgotten or left behind in His plans for creation. He doesn't want to give you only a sliver or a chunk of His kingdom; He promises that His Father—God—wants to give you the entire kingdom. Why? Because you're loved and priceless in His eyes.

Jesus, thank You for reminding me that You want to give me so much. Amen.

LIVES IN YOU

*"Christ lives in me. The life I now live in the
body, I live by faith in the Son of God, who
loved me and gave himself for me."*
GALATIANS 2:20 NIV

Unless you find a way to completely avoid it, there will probably be
a time in your life when you have to speak in front of others. Public
speaking is actually a very common fear, and a lot of people—even
celebrities who do it all the time—claim to get butterflies in their
stomach before a speaking event. A lot of people are scared of doing
it because most of the time they are doing it alone.

Think of anything you are scared of doing. Doing it alone
makes it one hundred times scarier. But thankfully, we don't have
to do it alone. When you accept Jesus, His Spirit lives in you, giving
you the ability to face and handle any circumstance.

Count on Him to give you strength and power and bravery
when you need it.

---

*Jesus, I need strength and power and
bravery for this:_____. Amen.*

LOVE THEM

There is neither Jew nor Gentile, neither
slave nor free, nor is there male and female,
for you are all one in Christ Jesus.
GALATIANS 3:28 NIV

It's such a good thing to celebrate everyone's differences. Look at how God created the world with such diversity and beauty. He wants you to be yourself and celebrate others. Especially within His church.

But sometimes certain people don't like the differences that set us apart. They make rules that make it hard for others to join a certain church or organization; they put down others and make them feel like they aren't good enough for the faith.

Jesus died for every single person: Jew, Gentile, slave, free, male, female—everyone! He wants everyone to have the chance to get to know Him. What Jesus did made us all equal and one in Him.

So always be kind to those who are different from you. Be the girl people know they can go to for acceptance and love like Jesus accepts and loves them.

Jesus, please help me to always be welcoming and loving to all I meet. You love them, Lord. So I will too. Amen.

GOOD WORKS

*For we are God's handiwork, created in
Christ Jesus to do good works, which God
prepared in advance for us to do.*
EPHESIANS 2:10 NIV

Do you have any idea what you want to do after high school? Do you want to go to college or travel, pick a job or volunteer somewhere? Planning for what comes next can be overwhelming, even when you're an adult. Especially when you have so many amazing choices and so many different interests.

The good news is you do have someone to help you narrow it down. God created you to do good works in the name of Jesus in an extra special way that only you can. He gave you talents and abilities that you can shape and grow to meet the needs around you. Jesus used His divine power on earth to follow the will of God, and you can use your own special power to do the same.

When you start looking and asking, God will be faithful in showing you what to do next.

---

*Jesus, let me see the doors that will lead to doing Your
good work in the way I was created to. Amen!*

UNSHAKABLE CORNERSTONE

Therefore the Lord God said: "Look, I have laid a stone in Zion, a tested stone, a precious cornerstone, a sure foundation; the one who believes will be unshakable."
ISAIAH 28:16 CSB

A house needs a strong foundation so it won't fall during a storm. When you learn a new instrument, it's important to learn notes before a full song. If you play a sport, you probably spend some time at practice going over certain plays so you're ready for anything come the big game. It's all about creating a strong foundation so under pressure you don't falter.

God knew His people would need a strong foundation to build their faith on through trials. So He sent the most perfect cornerstone—Jesus. Ephesians 2:20 (NIV) says the faith is "built on the foundation of the apostles and prophets, with Christ Jesus himself as the chief cornerstone." Because Jesus never changes, He is unshakable.

And with Him as your foundation, you become unshakable in the face of trials and disappointments because you know who is holding you up.

Jesus, thank You for always being there for me.
Let me lean on You for what I need. Amen.

THAT'S NOT ME!

I received mercy for this reason, so that in me, the worst of them, Christ Jesus might demonstrate his extraordinary patience as an example to those who would believe in him for eternal life.
1 Timothy 1:16 csb

Because of a bad mood, have you ever done or said something you never thought you would? Afterward, you probably felt guilty and wanted to shout, "That's not me!"

That meanness is not you. But it was your thoughts, your words, and your deeds. When you start spiraling into shame, it can be hard to pull yourself out of the not-good-enoughs and never-be-good-enoughs.

Jesus knew the struggle we'd have with sin and how we'd hurt one another. So He gave Himself to death to free the world of sin, creating a different path for you, one of forgiveness and kindness.

Before you let the sin in your life react, remember that mean reaction isn't you and doesn't have to be, because you were made new in Jesus (see 2 Corinthians 5:17).

Jesus, that's not me! Forgive me for things I've done and help me seek forgiveness from those I've hurt. Help me to react the way You would—in love.

LOVE DONE RIGHT

On hearing this, Jesus said, "It is not the healthy
who need a doctor, but the sick. But go and learn
what this means: 'I desire mercy, not sacrifice.' For
I have not come to call the righteous, but sinners."
MATTHEW 9:12–13 NIV

Watching a friend make decisions that cause pain in her life can be hard. It's easy to judge her for those decisions and choose to kick her out of your life. But Jesus demonstrates that He loves your friend just as much as He loves you. He came for her too. So unless being friends with her is dangerous, Jesus wants you to reach out and help her when she's in need. He doesn't want you to help only those who make the same decisions as you do or think the same way.

Jesus wants us to love others so much that they want to have a relationship with God. That love done right is done without judgment, full of grace and kindness. To do that you have to get close. And Jesus promises to be there to help and protect you.

Jesus, help me love others like You do. Amen.

THE IMPOSSIBLE

Jesus looked at them and said, "With man this is impossible, but with God all things are possible."
MATTHEW 19:26 NIV

"This is impossible!" You've thought this before. You've tried everything and nothing is working! When you're looking at a hard situation and see no answer or end in sight, all you want to do is scream in frustration and give up. Because in that moment, there is nothing you can do to make it right.

And that's where Jesus steps in. Because maybe this situation needs more of Him and less of you. When we finally give up trying to do it all on our own, and let Jesus take control, that's when impossible situations become possible.

Jesus did a lot of impossible things during His ministry. But He won't stop there. You can trust Him to do impossible things in your life today. You can trust Him.

Jesus, I know I can trust You to do the impossible.
I need to act like it and give up my control. Amen.

26

IMMANUEL

"Therefore the Lord himself will give you a sign: The virgin will conceive and give birth to a son, and will call him Immanuel."

Isaiah 7:14 niv

Immanuel. It's a word we usually hear at Christmas time, but it wasn't only written in the Gospels regarding His birth. Immanuel means "God with us," and the first mention of it is actually in the Old Testament. Jesus was fully human and fully divine as God's Son and a part of God as a whole. His plan of redemption for the world was mentioned way back in the book of Isaiah.

Jesus knew that to save the world He had to live in it, show His creation who He was, and explain what He meant to do. He had to show what life would be like when God is present.

"God with us." That is who Jesus is. John 1:14 (niv) says, "The Word became flesh and made his dwelling among us. We have seen his glory."

He showed His glory in His humanity and He showed His divinity by being willing to actually be with us.

Jesus, thank You for being with us back then and today. Amen.

JESUS WAS TEMPTED

Then Jesus was led by the Spirit into the
wilderness to be tempted by the devil.
MATTHEW 4:1 NIV

Cheating on your test. Lying to your parents. Making fun of others.
You are probably tempted every day to do things you don't want
to do, things you know are wrong. You are not alone in that. Jesus
was tempted on earth too. He was actually tempted by the devil
himself out in the desert. Check out Matthew 4 for the whole story.

When Jesus was tempted, He never once gave in. He knew
that God had His back and overcame each attack. Now the Lord
uses that encounter to prove to you that when you rely on Jesus,
temptations become bearable. Jesus gives a truth to rely on in the
face of temptation, a way to leave or a way to put a stop to it.

When you feel as if temptations are everywhere you turn, then
turn your gaze to Jesus. He will be there for you.

When I am faced with temptation, I will turn
to Your example, Jesus. Thank You.

GENTLY RESTORE

If someone is caught in a sin, you who live by
the Spirit should restore that person gently.
. . . Carry each other's burdens, and in this
way you will fulfill the law of Christ.
GALATIANS 6:1–2 NIV

Do you have a friend going through a hard time? It probably hasn't been fun watching her pull away from you or others. Or maybe. . .are you the one dealing with something difficult? Do you feel like no one could ever possibly understand you?

Jesus says that His followers need one another to stay faithful to Him. So when you see someone pulling away from the group or you yourself are isolating from others, remember that Jesus came to restore us. And He does this ever so gently. And He asks us to do the same for others.

Be gentle with your companions. Be gentle with yourself. Ask to offer help and always ask for help.

We were created to carry each other's burdens in the way Jesus did and continues to do so for all.

Jesus, I want to help others when they feel alone. And give me the strength and courage to ask for help when I need it. Amen.

LOVE HIM

"I see what you've done, your hard, hard work,
your refusal to quit. . . . I know your persistence,
your courage in my cause, that you never wear out.
But you walked away from your first love—why?
. . . Turn back! Recover your dear early love."
REVELATION 2:2–5 MSG

Jesus loves when you work hard to be good and when you don't quit in the face of temptations or when life gets hard. He especially loves it when you're courageous in His name to stand up for others and for what's right.

But He doesn't love it when you forget about *your love* for Him. He doesn't want you to get so caught up in what you need to do for Jesus that you forget why you're doing those things in the first place.

You want to do good because you love Jesus. If you feel burnt out or like you're going through the motions, come back to Him for rest and the reminders of why you are doing what you do.

Jesus, I want to come back to You and remember
Your love for me and my love for You. I love You!

PALM SUNDAY

*Rejoice greatly, Daughter Zion! Shout, Daughter
Jerusalem! See, your king comes to you,
righteous and victorious, lowly and riding on
a donkey, on a colt, the foal of a donkey.*
ZECHARIAH 9:9 NIV

Does this picture look familiar? That's because hundreds of years later Jesus fulfilled this prophecy by riding into Jerusalem on the back of a donkey, a week before His crucifixion. Check out Matthew 21 for that whole story!

The church celebrates this day as Palm Sunday, and you can also celebrate it as a prime example of the Lord keeping His promises to us.

God told the prophet Zechariah that Jesus would enter Jerusalem in humbleness and on a donkey—a long, long time before it actually happened. But God is faithful and never forgot what He said. Jesus shows you that God kept His promises back then and will keep His promises today.

---

*Jesus, thank You for always being an example of
God doing what He said He would do. Amen.*

WILL NOT PASS AWAY

"Heaven and earth will pass away,
but My words will not pass away."
MATTHEW 24:35 NLV

You've probably heard the saying "Everything must come to an end." And right now for you, it may feel like that's the only thing happening. Maybe you're graduating and leaving high school. Maybe you had to turn in your last project for your favorite after-school art class. Maybe it's your last year at your favorite summer camp. Or maybe your favorite show just aired its last heart-wrenching episode.

Jesus wants to remind you that everything in this life will someday pass away. That can be a scary and sad thought. But Jesus also wants you to know that the things that really matter won't ever go away—like His love for you and His promise of coming back.

His friendship with you will never end, never pass away.

Jesus, I am so happy You are coming back. Thank You for reminding me that Your love for me never ever ends. Amen.

BE EXALTED

*"Those who exalt themselves will be humbled,
and those who humble themselves will be exalted."*
LUKE 18:14 NIV

Jesus told a story of two men who came to the temple to pray. One was a Pharisee and the other was a tax collector. In those times, Pharisees were seen as very godly and holy people. Tax collectors. . .not so much. The Pharisee prayed about how he was so much better than everyone else—even better than the tax collector praying beside him.

But the tax collector asked God for forgiveness for himself for he knew he was a sinner.

Jesus said, "I tell you that this man, rather than the other, went home justified before God" (Luke 18:14 NIV). The tax collector came humbled before the Lord. He didn't try to make himself look better than anyone else. He recognized the things he did wrong and laid them before the Lord. This is how Jesus wants you to act.

Jesus asks you to always humble yourself before Him and other people, seeing that everyone needs forgiveness and light.

---

*Jesus, I humble myself before You. Please forgive
me and help me forgive others. Amen.*

PURPOSE FOR PAIN

They put them at his feet, and he healed them.
So the crowd was amazed when they saw those
unable to speak talking, the crippled restored,
the lame walking, and the blind seeing, and
they gave glory to the God of Israel.
MATTHEW 15:30–31 CSB

Many of Jesus' miracles during His time of ministry were healings. He helped the mute find their voices; He enabled those who couldn't walk to dance with joy; He gave sight to the blind.

Each person Jesus healed had a purpose for their pain. God didn't intend for people to withstand all this suffering, but because of this broken world, we will all endure it—physically and emotionally.

Yet Jesus is always with us in the trials, and He is working good things through them. We might not understand them now, but His plans and purposes will be revealed when He comes back with ultimate healing—when "there will be no more death or sorrow or crying or pain" (Revelation 21:4 NLV).

Jesus, while I pray for this healing today, I also pray for peace that You are with me, with everyone experiencing such heartache, and that there is a purpose here.

BECAUSE OF LOVE

But God proves his own love for us in that while
we were still sinners, Christ died for us.
ROMANS 5:8 CSB

Why did Christ die on the cross?

Because He loves us.

Every follower of Christ has thoughts and questions about the faith. The head craves logic and reason. Why would anyone choose to take the punishment of someone else? Would you take the failing grade of someone who never showed up to class, when you turned in every paper and aced every test?

Christ chose to take the world's punishment for sin because of love. It's so simple, yet hard to understand, and still completely the truth. You've probably heard this one before: "For God so loved the world that he gave his one and only Son. . ." (John 3:16 NIV).

Because of love, He died for us. Because of love, we can forgive ourselves and forgive others. Because of love, we get to spend eternity with Him.

Jesus, I may not understand everything about Your
sacrifice, but I do know that You chose death so we
didn't have to. You love us, Jesus, in our brokenness
and hurt with Your hope and healing. Amen.

DIG IN!

Jesus answered, "It is written: 'Man shall not live on bread alone, but on every word that comes from the mouth of God.'"
MATTHEW 4:4 NIV

If you could eat only one food for the rest of your life, what would you pick? The idea seems intriguing, but after a week of digging in, that favorite food will likely soon become something you never want to even smell again.

Jesus tells us that we can't eat only bread; we need other nutrients too. And He compares good nutrition to your faith life. You can't live on just one thing like bread; you can't live on just things given to you by this world alone. Jesus offers you so much more!

The Bible, along with helpful and trustworthy commentaries and study tools, can help you figure out what Jesus says is important. But that can't be done without the work. You have to dig in!

Jesus, help me find the motivation to dig into Your Word today! I want to learn more about You and Your promises. Amen.

BAD HABITS

*"You are to give him the name Jesus, because
he will save his people from their sins."*
MATTHEW 1:21 NIV

A habit is something you do over and over again so much that you don't notice it or know why. Most of these are harmless, like bouncing your knee in math class or eating the same cereal for breakfast each morning. But sometimes we fall into bad habits that are actually sins—like saying something to your friends to make them laugh at the new kid or lashing out at your parents when they just won't leave you alone.

Jesus came not only to forgive us of our bad habits but to save us from them. When you accept Jesus into your life, you're given the power to overcome temptations and break nasty habits. Some will be harder to rise above than others, and for some you may need to reach out to others you trust for help.

But Jesus is there because He's your rescuer—yesterday, today, and forever.

---

*Jesus, I don't want habits to hurt me or rule my life. Give me
wisdom and guidance on how to overcome them. Amen.*

FISHERS

Jesus said to them, "Follow Me.
I will make you fish for men!"
MARK 1:17 NLV

If you know anything about fishing, you know it takes a lot of patience. And maybe even a little boredom. But when a kid with his grandpa catches his first fish, the joy can't be denied. Casting out your line and waiting does pay off in the end.

What does it look like to be fishers of people? It means acting like Jesus, casting out kindness to everyone you meet. It's about sharing Him no matter how scary that can be. And it involves waiting—waiting for them to see how your life is different and waiting for them to have an interest in getting to know Jesus too.

Just as you'll be happy when someone finally takes ahold of what it would be like to have Jesus in their life, Jesus rejoices that someone else wants to get to know Him.

Jesus, I want others to know Your goodness. Help me to show
Your love in the best ways I can and to always be inclusive
and inviting to those who want to learn about You.

GRACE PERIOD

For it is by grace you have been saved, through faith—
and this is not from yourselves, it is the gift of God.
Ephesians 2:8 niv

The world record for the most overdue library book is 288 years. It was actually first borrowed in 1668! Libraries usually charged fines for books that were returned late. Can you imagine the size of that fine?!

Lucky for that guy, the library didn't charge a dime. And today, many libraries have a grace period before the fine kicks in on a late book. This is something that the library does purely for the benefit of their book borrowers.

God's plan is the same. We are given grace because He knew that we couldn't save ourselves. He knew we would fall short. So as a wonderful gift, and with no action on our part, Jesus came in and paid our fine, so we don't have to stress. That's grace!

Jesus, thank You for paying my fine. Because of this grace,
I want to do better in my own life to honor this gift. Amen.

YOU WILL BE COMFORTED

"Blessed are those who mourn,
for they will be comforted."
MATTHEW 5:4 NIV

In the Beatitudes, Jesus makes a long list of those who are blessed, and it may not make sense when you first read through it. Some of them make sense with the words *peacemaker* and *pure of heart* because we know we want to be those things. But how can someone who is meek, hungry, even persecuted, be blessed? When you're made fun of for your beliefs and the choices you make because of them, how is that a blessing?

Jesus answers, "Rejoice and be glad, because great is your reward in heaven" (Matthew 5:12 NIV). When you put Jesus first, there is a reward there: eternity with Him in heaven. And on earth, He promises you comfort.

It can be scary to stand strong for what you believe, but know that you join a long list of brave souls who have done the same, who all have Jesus right there by their side—just like you do.

Jesus, thank You for Your comfort. I will try my best
to see the blessing in this situation. Amen.

ALWAYS

Rejoice always, pray continually, give
thanks in all circumstances; for this is
God's will for you in Christ Jesus.
1 Thessalonians 5:16–18 niv

Let's be real. Something that is always constant in life is change. Seasons change; classes change every semester; friendships and circumstances never stay the same. Even our emotions (usually at a certain time of the month!) are sometimes all over the place.

But Jesus asks us to always praise Him and pray and say thank You in all situations. He asks this of us because it is God's will, which is what God knows to be the very best for us. We can praise and give thanks because Jesus never changes. His work on the cross and the promise He fulfilled will never go away.

So no matter what is changing in our own lives and leaving us spinning, we can know and be assured that Jesus is still the same. We can go to Him for peace when everything else feels out of control.

Jesus, life can feel so out of control with all of its constant
changes. Thank You for never changing! Amen.

PRAYERS OF GRIEF

"You will grieve, but your grief will turn to joy."
John 16:20 niv

You have lost someone dear to your heart. The thoughts that are in your head are angry and confused and rooted in a dark place called grief. It's lonely there. You've been doing the motions of life while caught in this fog. You've been lying in bed, praying that things were different.

Jesus is no stranger to grief. He asks you to pull closer to Him in these moments. Because He promises to be "near to those who have a broken heart. And He saves those who are broken in spirit" (Psalm 34:18 nlv). He promises hope that gives you meaning again, His company every day, and a peace that transcends understanding (see Philippians 4:7). And He promises that when He returns, all our grief will become joy, and there will be no more pain and no more tears.

In this season of loss, lean into His presence and promises and know that one day you will be joyful again.

Jesus, I bring this all to You—this hurt, this grief.
I lay it at Your feet to be transformed into joy.

BELIEVING IS SEEING

Jesus said, "Because you have seen me, you have believed. Blessed are those who have not seen and yet believe."

You just heard your bestie say something unbelievable in the hallway before school—something so crazy it couldn't possibly be real. But a little part of you still hopes that it is. Because life is so much better when you believe that the impossible can actually happen.

We don't have the chance to catch Jesus doing His miracles in person. Even if we can't see it happening, Jesus still asks us to have faith so strong that we don't need to see it; we just trust. We believe that what we ask and hope for will happen and we act like it too. Because He's come through for us before, and He will do it again.

With Jesus in your heart, you are one of the lucky ones, the blessed. Because you have believed without seeing.

Even on my hardest days, Jesus, I will keep trusting and believing, even when I haven't seen You move yet. Amen.

CHRIST IN CHARGE

*For the entire fullness of God's nature dwells bodily
in Christ, and you have been filled by him, who
is the head over every ruler and authority.*
Colossians 2:9–10 csb

You have to listen to what the bus driver says, then to your teachers in every classroom, and then to your coach and musical director after school. And then when you *finally* get home, you have to do what your parents tell you to. It can be frustrating to feel like everyone else is in charge of your entire life but you!

However, you have something inside you that's more powerful than all these. You follow Jesus, and He makes a home in your heart when you accept Him into your life. He rules over all, and He will let you know when you should follow rules because they're what's best for you and when to stand up for what is right when something seems unfair.

Christ is really the one in charge of your life. Listen to what He has to say.

---

*Jesus, I want You to be in charge! Thank You for reminding
me of my humbleness and power that come from You!*

OUT OF JESSE

On that day the root of Jesse will stand as a banner. . . . His resting place will be glorious.
ISAIAH 11:10 CSB

The words of Isaiah begin like this: "Then a shoot will grow from the stump of Jesse, and a branch from his roots will bear fruit. The Spirit of the LORD will rest on him—a Spirit of wisdom and understanding. . .of counsel and strength. . .of knowledge and of the fear of the LORD" (Isaiah 11:1–2 CSB).

We tend to skip over those long passages of names in the Bible, but in this instance, it proves why those are important too. Jesus—the one God promises to save His people—will come out of the line of Jesse. He'll bring with Him a peace the world has never known, with no hate or danger because "the land will be as full of the knowledge of the LORD as the sea is filled with water" (Isaiah 11:9 CSB). When we know Jesus fully, we know love, peace, perfect harmony.

Let's pray for that day to come.

Jesus, I look forward to the day all is made right and perfect harmony is the only thing the world will know. Amen.

THE VINE

*"I am the vine; you are the branches. The one
who remains in me and I in him produces much
fruit, because you can do nothing without me."*
JOHN 15:5 CSB

Keeping plants alive is a challenge. It can be hard to know how much water they need, what kind of soil they prefer. Some plants even need leaves taken off so they continue growing. You would think keeping something like a plant alive would be easy! But when you get it right and see your plant produce little flowers or your garden give back fruit and veggies, it's worth it.

Jesus views His believers the same way. He puts a lot of work and love into us, graciously giving us what we need while taking away and tenderly pruning what we don't. And when we remain in Him—the true vine—we produce fruit that resembles Christ. We show others the kindness, the goodness, the love of Jesus.

And maybe because others saw your fruit in action, they'll want to be a part of the vine too.

---

*Jesus, I want to produce the best fruit. Help me
to stay attached and close to You. Amen.*

LEFT UNDONE

He who began a good work in you will carry it
on to completion until the day of Christ Jesus.
PHILIPPIANS 1:6 NIV

You won't know what happens to the bubbling electric-blue liquid if you never finish the science experiment. A fun movie wouldn't be very good if the movie theater doesn't show the last twenty minutes. You definitely can't drive a car with only three wheels. Things won't be right unless they are finished completely. They can't be left undone.

Jesus never leaves anything undone. That includes you! He is working on you to become a reflection of Him and the person you were always meant to be. He has an amazing plan not only for you and your friends and family but the entire world. And He won't stop until it's completed. We can help Him in this plan by working on ourselves: following Him, reading His Word, and listening to His voice while we wait for His return.

Jesus, thank You that You never leave anything undone.
I am always growing to become more like You. Amen.

THE LIGHT

*"You are the light of the world. A town
built on a hill cannot be hidden."*
MATTHEW 5:14 NIV

You try talking to your friends about Jesus, but most of the time, you're met with half smiles and polite nods. Maybe some kids even make fun of you for sharing about Him. Neither outcome is encouraging when you hope they will say yes to Jesus right then and there.

Even Jesus knew that the best way to get people to come to Him is by action. Jesus performed miracles, and He spread kindness and goodness to all those around Him. His actions were a light that could not be hidden.

You have that power to do the same. Instead of only talking about Jesus, be sure to act like Him! Your kind actions will get others to start asking questions. You're the walking, living, breathing light of Jesus on earth. That kind of light can't be hidden.

---

*Jesus, I'm Your light! Help me to see situations
that need my kindness and my help so I can show
others who You are. And when they start asking
questions, I'll know exactly what to say. Amen.*

LAMB OF GOD

The next day John saw Jesus coming toward him and said, "Look, the Lamb of God, who takes away the sin of the world!"
JOHN 1:29 CSB

One of Jesus' names in the Bible is the Lamb of God. In the Old Testament, Israelites were told to spread the blood of a lamb above their doors to be passed over by the final devastating plague in Egypt that brought not only death but heartache and unspeakable grief.

Jesus' blood acted as the lamb's did back then. His blood allows judgment and death to pass over us because it paid the price of sin. All we need to do is accept His sacrifice for us. In the moment we do, we're rescued; we're given a peace that no matter what we've done, we will still have eternity with Him. With no more death, heartache, sadness, or grief.

"For the Lamb Who is in the center of the throne. . . . He will lead them to wells of the water of life. God will take away all tears from their eyes" (Revelation 7:17 NLV).

Jesus, thank You for being the Lamb of God and for Your sacrifice for me. Amen.

THE TEMPLE

*They replied, "It has taken forty-six years to build this
temple, and you are going to raise it in three days?"
But the temple he had spoken of was his body.*
JOHN 2:20–21 NIV

When Jesus told those in the temple that He was going to rebuild
the destroyed church in three days, people thought He was crazy.
And why wouldn't they? Their temple that had been built on earth
had taken them forty-six years!

But Jesus wasn't talking about the temple they were standing
in. He was talking about the entirety of believers coming together
as one, about His body being the physical placeholder for a divine
miracle about to take place. Jesus' body is the true temple.

He was torn down, dead and buried, but three days later He
came back to life. You have the blessing of knowing the end of
the story and can embrace His promises today, knowing that He's
already done the impossible and will do it again. Jesus is a temple
we can go to for good things, for all that we need.

---

*Jesus, You have done the impossible.
I believe in the resurrection. Amen!*

NO EXPIRATION DATE

In his great mercy he has given us new birth into
a living hope through the resurrection of Jesus
Christ from the dead, and into an inheritance
that can never perish, spoil or fade.
1 PETER 1:3–4 NIV

That sandwich you made for lunch weeks ago and forgot about is a hunk of green *something* at the bottom of your locker. Your favorite pair of jeans, once new, is now faded. That rush you got when you aced that test in history is forgotten about when you see your latest low grade in precalculus. A lot of things—even things that make us really happy—don't last long.

But the promise of eternity in heaven, a new life, with Jesus? That has no expiration date. We can still be "filled with an inexpressible and glorious joy" no matter what happens to us (1 Peter 1:8 NIV). Because even on earth we're still given the wonderful mercy and the amazing blessing of "receiving the end result of [our] faith" through our relationship with Him (1 Peter 1:9 NIV). There is no changing that!

Jesus, I am so glad I get to access that joy today
because of my friendship with You. Amen.

JOY!

"I have told you this so that my joy may be in you and that your joy may be complete."
JOHN 15:11 NIV

Ever had a day where everything goes wrong? You wake up late for school and miss the bus, you spill your iced coffee all over your backpack, and you say something totally embarrassing and awkward to the cutie beside you in band rehearsal. These little moments can add up to some hilarious stories down the line, but at the time they're definitely not fun.

Sadly, we have to deal with harder things too. Things that truly hurt us and stay with us for a long time. But Jesus says that He hears our cries, He sees our pain, and He's there with us through it all. He gives us a chance to feel His joy in every moment. Not just sometimes. All the time. You are never alone.

And His joy makes our own joy complete, whole, perfect. Whatever situation you're dealing with today, from embarrassment to heartache, you can find joy in the presence of Jesus.

Jesus, help me find Your joy in this earthly mess. Amen.

MERCY INSTEAD OF GUILT

Jesus said to her, "Neither do I say you are guilty.
Go on your way and do not sin again."
JOHN 8:11 NLV

You've been found out. Your loved ones know what you've done. Guilt covers your entire soul.

There was a woman who had committed adultery. She was thrown into the public square, shivering and scared of how the world would punish her. She faced her judgment alone, bare, full of shame.

Jesus, however, did not condemn her. Instead He said if there was anyone who's never sinned in the crowd surrounding her, they could throw stones. No one was sinless but Jesus, so they left Jesus to deal with the woman.

Instead of passing out the guilty verdict, Jesus handed her mercy. He told her to get up, go on her way, and to not sin again. That's really all we can do today too.

Mercy isn't a reason to "continue in sin so that grace may multiply" (Romans 6:1 CSB). Mercy shows us that we can do better and gives us the chance to try.

Jesus, I don't have to live in guilt. I can accept Your mercy and move forward, leaving that sin behind me in the dirt. Amen.

BABY SHOWER

"You will conceive and give birth to a son, and you are to call him Jesus. He will be great and will be called the Son of the Most High."
LUKE 1:31–32 NIV

A baby shower is usually the celebration of the family's first baby, and the mommy-to-be is given gifts and encouragement for the day. Mary, the mother of Jesus, didn't have such a party when she discovered she was pregnant. She was supposed to marry a man named Joseph. She was afraid people wouldn't understand what God had done.

But Mary was carrying Jesus, the Son of God. This baby was gonna grow up and do some mighty things. She knew that no matter what, she was highly favored, and she believed in the truth that "no word from God will ever fail" (Luke 1:37 NIV). This baby was going to change everyone's lives for the better. She just had to trust.

So let's shower Jesus in love. Because Mary truly delivered the greatest gift the world's ever seen!

Jesus, like Mary, I trust that Your plan will not fail. I love You and thank You for everything You've done for me. Amen.

THE BREAD OF LIFE

"I am the bread of life. . . . I am the living bread that came down from heaven. If anyone eats of this bread he will live forever."
JOHN 6:48, 51 CSB

Jesus fed five thousand people with only five loaves of bread and two small fish. Check out John 6:1–15 for that story. Every person that had listened to Him speak was stuffed, and there was still food left over. This wasn't just a miracle; Jesus used it as a metaphor for His own sacrifice. There was another type of bread that the world needed.

Jesus is the bread of life. He came down from heaven to give eternity to all creation. He is a sustainer. He fulfills our needs. Just as the five thousand with the bread He created, we have the chance to fill up on His goodness and blessings; and He never runs out! He still has some left over for those who haven't had the chance to get to Him yet.

Take a bite of the bread of life today—thank Him for what He has done.

Jesus, thank You for being my sustainer.
You know just what I need. Amen.

JESUS SEES YOU

When Jesus saw her, his heart broke.
He said to her, "Don't cry."
LUKE 7:13 MSG

We all want to be seen. We all have this deep desire for someone to know us, understand us, and love us within all our pain and all our darkness. During His time on earth, Jesus saw a grieving widow laying her son to rest. He not only saw her outwardly mourning; the Bible tells us that when He "*saw* her, his heart broke" (emphasis added). He noticed her and He deeply cared. That's how Jesus sees.

Other translations say that when He saw her, "his heart went out to her" (NIV), "He had loving-pity for her" (NLV), and "he had compassion on her" (CSB). But they all begin by saying that Jesus saw her.

Beloved, Jesus sees you in your heartache, and He is comforting you. He understands you completely and loves you so fully. Find safety, peace, and comfort in His arms today.

Jesus, thank You for seeing me. Thank You for
loving me. I find comfort in You today. Amen.

IMPROV!

*"For the Holy Spirit will teach you at
that time what you should say."*
LUKE 12:12 NIV

You've rehearsed. You've run through your lines with your castmates.
You're ready for the opening night of the school play. The lights
go up. Your scene's starting. You walk out on stage, open your
mouth, and. . .nothing comes out! You can't remember what you
were supposed to say.

But you've prepared for this moment too. With a little improv—
made-up lines and actions on the spot—you get to the point in the
scene where you're back on track. And the audience doesn't even
know you messed up.

Jesus promises us His Spirit will guide us in what to say when
we need help. This can be in a conversation with a friend who's
hurting, standing up for a stranger who needs your help, or even
telling someone all about the love of Jesus. We can prepare by
reading His Word and praying to Him, but He'll show us exactly
what to say in the moment. Even when at first we have no idea
what to say.

---

*Jesus, help me with this improv of life
when I need to speak for You.*

CALMNESS

*He got up, rebuked the wind and said to
the waves, "Quiet! Be still!" Then the wind
died down and it was completely calm.*
MARK 4:39 NIV

A group of friends were excited to go on their whale-watching trip. They prepared with cameras and sunscreen for the open sea. But one thing they didn't plan on was the rough waves their small boat endured. Thankfully, their captain was able to steer the boat against the waves and back to the safety of the shore.

Jesus' disciples didn't know what to do when a storm hit their boat on the sea. But on Jesus' command, the storm ceased and the sea grew calm. His followers declared, "Even the wind and the waves obey him!" (Mark 4:41 NIV).

Jesus has the ability to speak calmness into the storms of our lives. When we're tumbling in the waves of disbelief, anxiety, and hurt, He's there to command, "Be still!" For in this storm, He's working. All you have to do is rest in His peace and trust Him to guide you through.

---

*Jesus, I seek Your guidance. I seek Your peace.
Reach out Your hand and calm this storm! Amen.*

THE COMMANDMENTS

For what the law could not do since it was weakened by the flesh, God did. He condemned sin in the flesh by sending his own Son in the likeness of sinful flesh as a sin offering.

ROMANS 8:3 CSB

The Ten Commandments are instructions on how to love God and love others. While we try our best to follow these rules, there will be moments when we fall short.

That's when Jesus comes in. You already know that He never broke any of these commandments. He loved perfectly. He made sure "the law's requirement would be fulfilled in us who do not walk according to the flesh but according to the Spirit" (Romans 8:4 CSB). If you follow Him and accept His sacrifice, the debt is paid. The law is fulfilled in you because Jesus did it for you. Even if you falter and fail to love "perfectly."

Because of this mercy, we should always try our best to follow in His steps and love others how He loved us.

Jesus, I know the rules are there to protect me and protect others. I want to follow them and You. Amen.

DECLARE IT!

If you declare with your mouth, "Jesus is Lord," and believe in your heart that God raised him from the dead, you will be saved. For it is with your heart that you believe and are justified, and it is with your mouth that you profess your faith and are saved.
ROMANS 10:9–10 NIV

This is the scary part—truly believing that in Jesus Christ you're saved. Even adults who have been rooted in their faith their whole lives still sometimes have a hard time understanding they're not stuck in guilt, misery, and shame.

When you start to doubt you're saved, dig into your actions, reflecting the manner of Jesus. Keep on loving others. Tell them why you choose to move forward even when you're lost. When you say you follow Jesus and believe it in your heart, therefore following Him in your life, you will be saved.

You have a wonderful eternity waiting for you. You can rejoice in that truth even when the nights are long and the days are hard. Jesus is Lord! Declare it! You are His, and you are saved.

Jesus, I am saved! Thank You!

LONG-DISTANCE RUNNING

Start running—and never quit!... Keep your eyes on
Jesus, who both began and finished this race we're in.
HEBREWS 12:1–2 MSG

When it comes to running long distances, it isn't about speed.
Long-distance running is all about endurance and consistency.
Our walk with Jesus is the same. The writer of Hebrews believes
we are running a race toward eternity. And it could be a long one
with twisty turns and obstacles.

But we have Jesus to motivate us to keep going. "Study how he
did it. Because he never lost sight of where he was headed—that
exhilarating finish in and with God—he could put up with anything
along the way" (Hebrews 12:2 MSG).

Jesus understands exactly what you're going through. He knows
what it's like to grow up, get hurt, and fall down and what it feels
like to want to quit. But He didn't. He finished, and "now he's there,
in the place of honor, right alongside God" (Hebrews 12:2 MSG).

You can rely on Him when it gets tough to "shoot adrenaline
into your [soul]" (Hebrews 12:3 MSG).

Jesus, I want to keep running this race. Help me
build endurance and consistency. Amen.

ADDICTION

Jesus said to him, "Would you like to be healed?"
JOHN 5:6 NLV

Addiction is something so many people face, and there are a multitude of things that can be addicting, like social media, food, attention from others, drugs, alcohol, and sex. All can be harmful to our minds and our bodies—and harmful to our loved ones too.

There's no easy way out of addiction. We must really want to be healed. And Jesus asks us that today—do you want to be healed?

Jesus has come to renew us. With the help of programs and support lines and big-hearted volunteers, there are ways to break addictions. Alongside a steady relationship and reliance on Jesus, you can say, "Yes, I want to be healed." Know that with His help and trusting the long process of recovery, it may not get easier, but it will get better. He will be with you every step of the way.

Jesus, I want to be healed. I want to rely on You alone. Be with me. When it gets hard, I'll cling to You and the loved ones You've placed in my life who want the best for me. Amen.

VICTORY OVER DEATH

But thanks be to God, who gives us the
victory through our Lord Jesus Christ!
1 Corinthians 15:57 csb

"Where, death, is your victory? Where, death, is your sting?" (1 Corinthians 15:55 csb). Jesus Christ conquered death by dying on the cross and rising from the dead three days later, in His divine glory.

But the real miracle of His resurrection was more than that. His death was sacrificial. It paid the price of sin. He took the sin of the world as His own and died because of it, for us, because He loves us so. But death could not hold Him. Jesus Christ, being the absolute embodiment of perfect love, fought death with two scarred hands and won. Love is more powerful.

This doesn't mean we'll never die. But this should bring a comfort that we have no need to fear death because we know we'll have eternity in heaven because of the sacrifice He made.

Jesus, thank You for the victory over death! When I think
about death and I'm afraid, remind me that You have
fought death and won. I have no reason to fear. Amen.

NO FEAR IN LOVE

There is no fear in love. But perfect love drives out fear, because fear has to do with punishment.
1 JOHN 4:18 NIV

When you read the Old Testament, you may only see "thou shalt not" and then a whole lot of punishments that follow. The God followers of that time sure had plenty of rules to wrap their heads around.

And some churches still have that mindset today—that God is a punisher. It's no wonder some people were and are scared of God.

But Jesus brought forth a whole new view of God. Instead of a punisher, Jesus emphasized that God is love. As the writer of 1 John 4:18 (NIV) states, "There is no fear in love. . . . Because fear has to do with punishment." We are not created or called to condemn others but to show them Christlike love. And this kind of love has nothing to do with fear. It actually destroys fear. That's what perfect love can do. And you are capable of this perfect love.

Jesus, I want to show others perfect love.
Help me to see how I can do that. Amen.

THIS IS MY BODY

*While they were eating, Jesus took bread, and when
he had given thanks, he broke it and gave it to his
disciples, saying, "Take and eat; this is my body."*
MATTHEW 26:26 NIV

Many churches practice a tradition called communion. This is when a believer practices what Jesus and His disciples did during the Last Supper. They break bread and drink wine or juice in remembrance of what Jesus has done. If you've taken communion many times, it can be easy to just go through the motions, but what does this act actually mean?

Jesus took bread, broke it, and gave a piece to each of His followers. He told them that it was His body, broken for them. Previously, "Jesus declared, 'I am the bread of life. Whoever comes to me will never go hungry'" (John 6:35 NIV). Jesus provides everything we need through the act of His broken body on the cross. And we're allowed and encouraged to accept that sacrifice. Jesus wants to provide salvation to His creation.

---

*Jesus, thank You for Your sacrifice. I may not understand
everything yet, but I know I can trust You. Amen.*

THIS IS MY BLOOD

"For this is my blood of the covenant, which is poured out for many for the forgiveness of sins."
MATTHEW 26:28 CSB

During the Last Supper, Jesus took a cup and asked every one of His followers to drink from it. He said that this was His blood, spilled for the forgiveness of sins. Whoa! No light dinner conversation at this table. And the disciples were confused. What did their Savior mean?

The price of sin is death. Jesus paid that price with His own blood, His own life, so our sins would be forgiven. He gave His life willingly; He gave His blood lovingly—so we, His beloved, would never have to face eternity without Him. Communion can be a reminder of this act of ultimate love.

If you choose to partake in communion, remember that there's a promise in it—one day we will see Jesus in all His glory in our forever home with Him.

Jesus, thank You. I trust that You love me and keep Your promises. I accept them both today. Amen.

THE PERFECT TABERNACLE

*Christ has appeared as a high priest of the
good things that have come. In the greater
and more perfect tabernacle not made with
hands (that is, not of this creation).*
HEBREWS 9:11 CSB

No matter how well buildings are built, they are not meant to stand forever. Can you imagine eating dinner, and a piece of your living room ceiling falls to the floor!? Buildings—from the smallest homes to the biggest skyscrapers—take upkeep to stay in tip-top shape.

Back in the Old Testament, God's Spirit only resided in one place—the tabernacle. Only high priests could enter it. That's why God sent Jesus. This true High Priest, through His sacrifice, broke down the walls of this tabernacle and picked the perfect place for God's Spirit to reside—in each of His followers, including you!

Because of Jesus, we no longer have to go to a special place to commune with our Savior. He's with us every moment of every day in the perfect tabernacle—you! You can truly experience the "good things that have come."

---

*Jesus, You're always with me. Whenever I need You,
I can just say the word and You're there. Thank You!*

BE FILLED

*Jesus took the five loaves of bread and two
fish. . . . They all ate and were filled. After that the
followers picked up twelve baskets full of pieces of
bread and fish. About five thousand men ate the bread.*
MARK 6:41–44 NLV

You probably know this story. . .Jesus fed five thousand people with
a little boy's lunch. It's one of Jesus' biggest miracles. But let's look
a little deeper. Scripture says the people who ate this meal "were
filled." That meant they were satisfied with what the Lord had done
in a situation that at first seemed impossible.

There will be times in life when Jesus will ask you to step into
a situation with limited resources. You will think you don't have
the talent, money, or supplies to finish (or even start!) what Jesus
has asked you to do.

Jesus will always help you find ways to get what you need to
accomplish what He calls you to do. Just let yourself be filled with
His presence. You and others will be satisfied and full. And you
may have blessings left over to keep on sharing His goodness.

Jesus, You make impossible things possible. Thank You!

NIGHT-LIGHT

Jesus spoke to them again: "I am the light of the world. Anyone who follows me will never walk in the darkness but will have the light of life."

JOHN 8:12 CSB

When a little child is sleeping alone and feels scared of the dark, a loved one may put a night-light in their room to make them feel safe. Even the smallest amount of light chases away darkness.

Jesus calls Himself the light of the world. And He makes the most wonderful promise that in this dark world if we have Him, we'll always have light. This light can make situations clearer, give you hope to press on, and create a place where you feel safe. And this light comes from Him who lives within you.

Even the smallest amount of light, even faith as small as a mustard seed (see Luke 17:5–6) can chase away the darkness. Trust that when you look around and see only the dark, Jesus is there to light the way.

Jesus, when I am in darkness, I will rely on You to light the way. Amen.

SHINE

For you were once darkness, but now you are
light in the Lord. Walk as children of light.
Ephesians 5:8 csb

You have plugged the light of Jesus into your life. You are shining. And hopefully others are seeing you shine this light all around you. You are kind to others. Your actions speak love. That's what Jesus wants you to do!

As a follower of Him, you are a reflection of Him. You are filled with the Holy Spirit, and by acting toward others the way Jesus would act, we will see this light diminish darkness in so many aspects of our lives.

You are living, breathing light for the world. It can be a big responsibility, and sometimes you'll get burned out. You may not feel able to be the bright light that day. But no worries! That means you're up for a refill. You have Jesus on your side to refill your lamp and your heart.

Jesus, I want to be a light for others. Help me to shine!

A LIVING STONE

As you come to him, a living stone—rejected by
people but chosen and honored by God—you
yourselves, as living stones, a spiritual house, are
being built to be a holy priesthood to offer spiritual
sacrifices acceptable to God through Jesus Christ.
1 PETER 2:4–5 CSB

C. S. Lewis states that God is working on you so you become a palace that He intends to come live in Himself. What a powerful image, one that's talked about in 1 Peter too. As followers of Christ, we're a spiritual house, continually being built through life's circumstances.

Our bodies have become "livable" through the power of Jesus and what He's done for us. Jesus broke down the barrier between God and His people on the cross. You never have to live without Him. You'll always be accepted by Him. He's living with you through it all. He wants you to love the body you have and take care of it because it is becoming a beautiful palace.

Jesus, I want to be a palace. I want You to be proud
of where You live. Reside in me and help me make
good decisions regarding my body. Amen.

SO LOVED

"For God so loved the world that He gave His only Son. Whoever puts his trust in God's Son will not be lost but will have life that lasts forever."

JOHN 3:16 NLV

Agape love is the kind of love that takes action. It is giving up your money to the charity you believe in. It is giving your time to someone who needs your friendship. It's giving up what you want to care for another. It has no expectations.

It's hard to see examples of this kind if we aren't looking. But we can look at scripture to see an ultimate act of agape love. Jesus, God's Son, died on the cross and paid the debt for humanity's sins. Why did He do this? Because of love. Because "God so loved the world. . ."

Jesus wants us to act on this agape love today. Not because of a duty or an oath but because our actions are based out of love for Him, for ourselves, and for others.

Jesus, I want to have agape love for this world and the people You have put in my life. Help me to do this with an open heart. Amen.

TAKE THE BLAME

Therefore, he is able to save completely
those who come to God through him, since
he always lives to intercede for them.
HEBREWS 7:25 CSB

Ever had somebody take the blame for you? Maybe your brave brother took the time-out when it came to the broken vase on the kitchen floor, or your friend told your teacher she was the only one who took the answers to the test from his desk. Hopefully, the act of someone taking the blame for you left you completely grateful and you promised your friends, yourself, and God that you wouldn't do it again.

Jesus doesn't make sacrifices every day for what we get wrong. His sacrifice once and for all paid for the world's sins (see Hebrews 7:27). He took the blame even though He was innocent. We have to try our best to be more like Him, and when we do mess up, we can know that He is there to offer forgiveness.

Jesus, thank You for taking the blame. Because of this,
I want to be the best person I can be, someone like You!

CALM IN THE STORM

*A furious squall came up, and the waves broke
over the boat, so that it was nearly swamped.
Jesus was in the stern, sleeping on a cushion.*
MARK 4:37–38 NIV

Before the glorious moment of Jesus calming the storm and the sea, He was taking a nap. In this scripture, we get the image of a terrible storm at sea, a boat being thrown back and forth in the waves, and the disciples terrified that they will drown. And in the very next line, we get an image of Jesus sleeping.

That truly is a peace that surpasses all understanding—to be in the midst of a storm but still find rest. But guess what? We have that ability too. Jesus resides within us and promises to be with us during every storm, every moment that feels like it will capsize our life. When we really need it, we can always reach out to Him for understanding, peace, and true rest to face what will come next.

---

*Jesus, I rest in You. I want that perfect peace. I know that
with You by my side I can find calm in the storm. Amen.*

WHY WORRY?

"Why should you worry about clothes? Think how
the flowers grow. They do not work or make cloth.
But I tell you that Solomon in all his greatness
was not dressed as well as one of these flowers."
MATTHEW 6:28–29 NLV

If you made a list of what worries you the most, would clothes be near the top of the list? Usually worrying about what we wear is actually worrying about what other people think of us. You ask yourself if your favorite sweatshirt is actually cool or if your homecoming dress is pretty enough.

The answer should be that if you like it, you should wear it! But when we get caught up in what other people think of us, we don't always make it that easy.

Jesus lets us know that we shouldn't worry about that. The flowers grow just as God intended, and not even Solomon, one of the richest men in history, was as well dressed. You were made to be you, and God didn't intend you to worry about that or what you will wear. He will care for you in all ways.

Dear Jesus, thank You for the reminder. Why worry?

WHY ME?

*"Neither this man nor his parents sinned,"
said Jesus, "but this happened so that the
works of God might be displayed in him."*
JOHN 9:3 NIV

When something bad happens to us, we may ask the dreaded question "Why me?" You may pepper your parents or mentor or God with questions like, "Did I do something wrong?" or "Do I really deserve this?"

Jesus healed a man who was blind. That man may have asked himself that dreaded question about being blind: "Why me?" Some people thought he was blind because either he or his parents sinned. Those rumors may have gotten to him. He may have started to think that he did do something to deserve blindness. But Jesus said that wasn't the answer. No one sinned. Instead, because of this man's own hardship, he was able to allow Jesus to display God's power.

We may not understand why something bad happens to us, but we can be sure that if we let Him, Jesus will use it for good. We just have to trust Him.

---

*Jesus, I know You will use this hardship for my
good. Help me trust You in these moments.*

ANXIETY

He began to have much sorrow and a heavy heart.
MATTHEW 26:37 NLV

Anxiety is something so many of us deal with today. It can be immobilizing. You may not want to leave your bed. It can be deafening. You can't hear encouragement over the negativity it is spewing in your mind. It can be heartbreaking. You feel lost and unsure and alone.

Jesus dealt with anxiety too. He felt the same desperate and dark emotions you're feeling. Before His time on the cross, Jesus spent a night in a garden, praying, crying out to God about how scared He was. He even prayed for His Father to change the circumstances, to find another way (see Matthew 26:39). Have you prayed those words to your heavenly Father?

When He realized that He had to go on, Jesus found the strength to move forward and perform an act of ultimate love. Jesus knows how it feels to deal with anxiety. You're not alone in these feelings. You can find rest and peace in Him.

Jesus, I need relief from this. I come to You now. Amen.

EYES ON JESUS

*I've got my eye on the goal, where God is
beckoning us onward—to Jesus. I'm off and
running, and I'm not turning back.*
PHILIPPIANS 3:13–14 MSG

As followers of Jesus, we are called to look forward instead of
backward. But the past has a way of creeping back into our present
and affecting how we view our future. We make mistakes—we
sin—and the enemy wants nothing more than to keep us there in
that cycle of guilt and shame. God never wants us to stay in that
muddy puddle of discouragement. We are meant for forgiveness.
We are meant to move forward toward Jesus.

Let go of your past today. Let go of that pain, embarrassment,
and shame. Turn your eyes toward Jesus. Trust that He has dealt
with your sin, He has healed your hurt, and you are made new
(see Ephesians 4:24). You don't have to be who you were, and you
don't have to be controlled by what you have done. You are His.

Jesus, I am off and running! And I am not turning back!

FRAGRANCE

For to God we are the fragrance of Christ
among those who are being saved and
among those who are perishing.
2 Corinthians 2:15 csb

Our sense of smell is closely linked to our memories. That's why it always feels like a Sunday when you smell the perfume your mom wears to church, or you fill up with good feelings when you experience that after-rain smell that takes you back to your elementary school's playground. Fragrance takes us back, tells stories, and invokes powerful emotions.

God tells us that we are the fragrance of Christ. We are the lingering example of His love for others. We are the walking, breathing, talking memory of Jesus for those around us. We want to only bring good smells and good memories to those who don't know Jesus yet. So we can show that He is someone well worth following and making memories with.

Jesus, thank You that we get the chance to
remember so many good things. I want to be a
good memory of You to everyone around me.

FOUR NAMES

And he will be called Wonderful Counselor,
Mighty God, Everlasting Father, Prince of Peace.
ISAIAH 9:6 NIV

Jesus has many names in the Bible. Here are four of them, and these were given to Him before He was even born! Let's take a look at them and what they mean.

Wonderful Counselor—Jesus is someone you can lean on in times of trouble and someone who will give you helpful and truthful advice. And He's always there.

Mighty God—Jesus is 100 percent God. He is all-powerful and all-knowing.

Everlasting Father—Jesus cares for you because you are His own. And this love never ever goes away.

Prince of Peace—Nothing and no one can give you the same peace that Jesus offers, a perfect peace that has no expectations.

Are there any other names for Jesus you can think of off the top of your head? What do they mean to you?

Jesus, thank You for being Wonderful Counselor,
Mighty God, Everlasting Father, and Prince of
Peace. I truly can rely on You for anything.

IN THE BEGINNING

"Bethlehem Ephrathah, you are too little to be among the family groups of Judah. But from you One will come who will rule for Me in Israel. His coming was planned long ago, from the beginning."

MICAH 5:2 NLV

Let's go all the way back to the garden of Eden. Humanity sinned. Sin separated us from God—for what looked like forever. But God had a plan. A plan that He had in place way before He said, "Let there be light" (Genesis 1:3 NIV).

A ruler would come out of a small town called Bethlehem. A ruler who would lead for God in Israel. It can be easy to view God as this all-powerful being who created the world and then took a step back once we disobeyed Him. But that isn't true. Since that very moment God was preparing His Son to destroy death and overcome the sin in our lives.

He never once stopped thinking of us. Jesus is proof of that.

In the beginning, Jesus, You were there, already working on a way to bring me back to You. Thank You!

BETTER PLANS

All this took place to fulfill what the Lord had said through the prophet: "The virgin will conceive and give birth to a son, and they will call him Immanuel" (which means "God with us").
MATTHEW 1:22–23 NIV

All Joseph wanted was his happily-ever-after. But the unbelievable happened. . .his fiancée was pregnant with a child he knew wasn't his, and she claimed it was the Savior. Of course he didn't believe her.

But God had picked Joseph to be Jesus' father because Joseph was a good man. And an angel appeared to Joseph in a dream, quoting what Isaiah prophesied back in the Old Testament. Joseph would have heard of this before. And what a shock it must have been to know that he was now an important part of that story.

Jesus, more often than not, has plans for us that don't line up exactly with what we want. But when we trust Him, we find that those plans are usually better than we can imagine. We become a part of a story that isn't only about us but about Him.

Jesus, instead of butting heads, help me to trust You when my plan changes. Amen.

ON THE BEHALF OF ANOTHER

When Jesus saw their faith, he said to the
paralyzed man, "Son, your sins are forgiven."
MARK 2:5 NIV

A group of friends, so desperate to help their paralyzed friend, climbed on top of a roof, made an opening, and lowered their friend to the feet of Jesus. They had faith that Jesus had the power to heal him, and because of this faith, not only was he healed but first the man's sins were forgiven.

We have the power to come to Jesus on behalf of another. We have power in the prayer of faith that asks Jesus to reach out to someone we love, to show them who He is, to show them love. Maybe Jesus will reveal Himself to them in a very real way. Or maybe Jesus will show you what your friend needs, what you can do to help, and what you should say to them.

But first you must lay your friend at the feet of Jesus in faith and humbleness.

Jesus, I lift my friends up to You. Show me
how to care for them. Amen.

FEELS A LOT LIKE CHRISTMAS

While they were there, the time came for her to give birth. She gave birth to a son, her firstborn. She wrapped him in a blanket and laid him in a manger, because there was no room in the hostel.

LUKE 2:6–7 MSG

Snow has fallen. Houses are aglow with colorful lights. You've made a list of presents to get for your friends and family, and a list for what you hope will be under the tree for you come that wonderful morning. But while we're celebrating this great season, let's not forget what it's really about: the birth of our Savior and His humble beginnings in a manger, the scene of animals in a stable, surrounding a loving couple as they gaze at their baby who brings the promise of redemption. It is a scene of peace, love, and excitement.

Hmmm. . .peace, love, and excitement. . .that feels a lot like Christmas, but they're also three things we can feel all year long when it comes to thoughts of our Savior.

Jesus, no matter what time of the year, I can remember the peace, love, and excitement that You bring. Amen.

FREEDOM

*"So if the Son sets you free, you are
free through and through."*
JOHN 8:36 MSG

A dog was chained to the same tree day after day. He knew exactly how far he could go until the chain held him back. One day, his kind new owner took off his chains. The old dog was free! But then the dog went to the place where the end of his chain usually stopped him—and froze. He didn't think he could move forward anymore. Even though the chains were gone.

We can be the same. We can spend so much time stuck in a certain state of mind or a specific sin that we don't think we can ever be free. But Jesus, your friend and Savior, has already broken the chains off you. You are free, even if you don't feel like it. So take that step. Pass the point of comfort and security. You will experience the freedom Jesus promised you.

I want to experience freedom, Jesus. Help me take that step.

HE WON!

"God has raised up His Son Jesus and has sent Him to you first to give God's favor to each of you who will turn away from his sinful ways."

ACTS 3:26 NLV

Some people thought Jesus was going to be a mighty warrior, bringing freedom to Israel as a country. But Jesus wasn't born a prince or the son of a military leader. He didn't enter Jerusalem on a warhorse but on a donkey. He preached against fighting, promoting love instead. In a lot of ways, Jesus wasn't what the world wanted.

But Jesus was what the world needed. Jesus was "raised up" in so many ways to fulfill God's plan of the world's redemption. Jesus did end up fighting a battle. He fought sin on the cross and death in the grave. And three days later, He rose again, victorious. He won the only battle that truly mattered; He broke sin's hold on us.

You are in God's favor because of what Jesus has done. You have the power to turn from your sinful ways and choose to follow Jesus into goodness and light.

Thank You, Jesus, for what You've done. You won!

BE THE DIFFERENCE

For I am not ashamed of the gospel, because it is the power of God for salvation to everyone who believes.
ROMANS 1:16 CSB

When you look at how some of those who claim they're Christians treat others, do you feel ashamed? Are you afraid to lump yourself in with those who definitely don't treat others the way Jesus would? We don't want to associate with those who misuse God's name and Jesus' teachings, but if we are embarrassed to say we follow Christ, how will anyone know what being like Jesus is actually like?

Do not be ashamed of the gospel. Don't be afraid to say you believe in Jesus and the cross. You have the chance to show the world what real love looks like. You can be the difference to those who have been hurt by the church and others. You can show others that Jesus is not about hate or judgment but all about love and forgiveness.

Jesus, I don't want to be embarrassed. I want to share with the world what You have done for me.

FOLLOW ME

"Whoever serves me must follow me;
and where I am, my servant also will be."
JOHN 12:26 NIV

You probably played the game follow-the-leader when you were little. Your friend was the leader, and you had to do everything she did. Now that you're older, you probably experience another sort of game of follow-the-leader. But this one is much more real-life. Do you follow your older sibling to know what school clubs to join? Do you follow the popular kids at school to know who to talk to? Do you follow certain others to know how to act? Are any one of them your leader?

A disciple is someone who follows. There was a reason "Jesus said to them, 'Follow Me'" (Mark 1:17 NLV). There should only be one person you're a disciple of, and that's Jesus. Where He goes, you should go. What He does, you should do. He will never lead you astray. He will lead you to become the person you were meant to be in Him.

Jesus, check my heart. Who am I following?
I want to be a disciple of You.

PURE JOY

Whatever I have, wherever I am, I can make it through
anything in the One who makes me who I am.
PHILIPPIANS 4:12–13 MSG

What do you feel that you need to be happy? The starting position on your team? The lead in the musical? Your crush? Those things are great, and they are wonderful blessings, but do they have the power to give you true, pure joy?

Jesus promises that no matter what we have or where we are in life, we can make it through anything if we rely on Him—because Jesus is the reason we are who we are. He is the reason for our blessings and the greatest promise of all—eternity with Him. When we focus on the good things Jesus gives us, we find true joy.

With Jesus as our focus, some of the good things we once thought were most important will still make us happy, but our whole life will not depend upon them.

Whatever life gives me or takes away, Jesus,
I will find contentment and joy in You.

IN THE BUSINESS OF HEALING

Jesus heard it and said to them, "People who are well
do not need a doctor. Only those who are sick need
a doctor. I have not come to call those who are right
with God. I have come to call those who are sinners."

MARK 2:17 NLV

You really want this job, so you tell the interviewer all the really good stuff. At the end, you give yourself a pat on the back. You made yourself look great!

Jesus doesn't want us to pretend the worst parts of ourselves don't exist. We're needy. We're hurting. We are sometimes mean. And we are lonely. He wants those parts of you. Because Jesus is in the business of healing.

Just as a doctor helps sick people, Jesus saves those who need saving. When we come clean with ourselves that we're not perfect and we show Jesus our imperfections, He gets to work. This is why He came. To make us whole in Him and healthy in spirit.

Jesus, I'm sorry that I've been afraid to show You
my real self. Thank You for not ever condemning
me. You will heal me if I let You. Amen.

FAMILIAR WITH YOUR PAIN

A man of suffering, and familiar with pain.
ISAIAH 53:3 NIV

How can the Son of God know the pain you have gone through, the pain you are going through? A pain caused by your own choices...or pain that has no meaning or explanation, pain you did nothing to cause.

The Bible tells us Jesus was "a man who suffered, who knew pain firsthand" (Isaiah 53:3 MSG). He is no stranger to betrayal, loneliness, heartache, grief, temptation, or hurt. He knew all types of pain. And from His safety in heaven, He knew He was going to experience those hard things, and still He chose to come down. Because He needed to create an eternity where those things will no longer exist.

As alone as you may feel in this circumstance, Jesus is familiar with your pain. He understands, and He offers comfort. He wants to give you peace. And maybe in that realization, you find it—strength to push on or strength to fully rest.

Jesus, I know You go before me and would never leave me in this pain. I need to know what to do next.

JESUS KNOWS WE'RE ANXIOUS

Cast all your anxiety on him because he cares for you.
1 PETER 5:7 NIV

We worry. It's a part of life. Maybe you have had some thoughts like these: *What are my friends going to think of me? Why did I say something so silly? Do they even like me?* These thoughts come from anxiety! Anxiety doesn't help you in any way; it only seeks to drag you out of the moment and into your head.

Jesus provides a way out of these thoughts. Have a moment with Him, one where you simply speak your mind. Say whatever you need to; He will understand. Once you've spoken what you need to, give it up to Him. Feel your chest begin to unclench, and allow your heart to fully beat as you simply accept life as it is. The peace of Jesus will eventually win out.

Jesus, my brain is moving too quickly. Please help me breathe in Your presence and find Your peace.

NOTHING CAN BEAT JESUS' LOVE

For I am convinced that neither death nor life. . .neither the present nor the future, nor any powers. . .nor anything else in all creation, will be able to separate us from the love of God that is in Christ Jesus our Lord.
ROMANS 8:38–39 NIV

Despite having the best intentions, people's love will let us down. It doesn't matter if she's your best friend or he's a stranger on the internet, everyone will eventually do or say something that isn't loving and hurts us deeply. That doesn't mean that we deserved it or that they're bad people; it means that we're all flawed and can't love others perfectly.

But there is a love that we can rely on, and that is the love of Jesus. He may not always love us the way that we think He should, but He ALWAYS loves us the way that we need.

And this isn't the commitment of a person, able to be broken or backed out on. This is the promise of Jesus, who is always faithful. Nothing can beat His love!

---

*Jesus, thank You for loving me completely.
I am so grateful to be able to trust You.*

SHARE OR NOT TO SHARE

If we live in the light as He is in the light, we share what we have in God with each other. And the blood of Jesus Christ, His Son, makes our lives clean from all sin.

1 John 1:7 nlv

You were made to share your time, your energy, and your life with others when you can, and it's healthy to do so. Sharing our lives can bring amazing opportunities but also some nerve-racking situations.

If we walk in the light, meaning we walk in the way of Jesus, we're bound to show it. Ever heard the song "This Little Light of Mine"? It's true! We share what we have inside us with one another, and it can't be hidden.

Because of Jesus and His forgiveness of our sins, you don't have to be afraid to share your light with others. Even the tiniest flame lights up the dark. Trust Him! You got this!

Dear Jesus, sharing my life with others can be scary. But I want to be a beacon of Your light! Help me see ways to connect with others.

CHANGE YOUR LIFE

This Isaiah-prophesied revelation came
to life in Galilee the moment Jesus
started preaching. . . . "Change your
life. God's kingdom is here."
MATTHEW 4:17 MSG

It was time. Just as the prophet Isaiah said, Jesus went to the "land of Zebulun, land of Naphtali, road to the sea, over Jordan" (Matthew 4:15 MSG) and His ministry began. In the final verses of Matthew, we see Jesus teach, proclaim the good news, and heal those with diseases and in pain. But you know what the people—the "people sitting out their lives in the dark" (Matthew 4:16 MSG)—actually saw?

They "saw a huge light" (Matthew 4:16 MSG). They "watched the sun come up" (Matthew 4:16 MSG). What beautiful imagery. Jesus is the sun, rising to chase away darkness, to bring newness to an old world battered by sin. He was God's kingdom on earth, telling others it was time to change their lives.

And He tells you today to change your life. For He is closer than you could even imagine—living in your heart.

Jesus, You changed my life. Thank You!

JESUS WALKS ON WATER

"Take courage! It is I. Don't be afraid."
Matthew 14:27 NIV

Some of Jesus' disciples were skilled fishermen. They fished on the Sea of Galilee and probably experienced plenty of storms. But you can bet none of them had ever seen someone walk on water. When they saw Jesus walking on the sea, they were terrified at first. But Jesus immediately told them not to be afraid. Because it was Him.

Jesus has the ability to give you courage at the mention of His name. When you feel scared and you have no idea what to do, say His name. *Jesus.* When you feel stuck, trapped, unsure where to go in the storm, say His name. *Jesus.* He chases away darkness. He walks on water. He encourages you to do the same.

If there is something you know Jesus is asking you to do but you still have fear, focus on Him. Take a deep breath. Say His name. *Jesus.* And step out onto the waves.

Jesus.

JESUS RESCUES PETER

Immediately Jesus reached out his hand and caught him. "You of little faith," he said, "why did you doubt?"
MATTHEW 14:31 NIV

The first time you rode a bike without training wheels, did you glide happily along, then all of a sudden, you remembered you were doing it alone? Did you tumble out of balance when you told yourself there was no way you could do it?

Peter started sinking the moment he took his eyes off Jesus. He was walking on water! But instead of focusing on his Savior, his attention turned to the storm he was in and the waves he was struggling through. Peter was confident in Jesus, but he let the darkness around him distract him. That's when he started sinking.

We've probably all been in hard times when we let our problems take our attention away from the one who rescues us from it all. Thankfully, just like Peter, we have Jesus, who will always be there to pull us from the storm, out of the waves, and into His arms.

Jesus, I'm sorry for taking my eyes off You. I take Your hand now, to pull me from these waves.

THE BRIDGE TO GOD

For there is one God and one mediator between
God and mankind, the man Christ Jesus, who
gave himself as a ransom for all people.
1 Timothy 2:5–6 niv

God wants to give everyone a chance to experience His love. He wants to give His creation "peaceful and quiet lives" (1 Timothy 2:2 niv). That may sound boring, but God just means that He never intended us to bear such stress and heartache in a world filled with hate and injustice. That's why He made the plan to fix it.

Jesus is our mediator. He is the one who bridged the gap that separated us from God because of sin. His sacrifice removed the veil (2 Corinthians 3:15–17) so we can see God clearly, commune with Him consistently, and spend eternity with Him. Because of Jesus, we don't have to do it all on our own; we have an actual relationship with our Creator.

Jesus, thank You for doing what humanity couldn't—connecting
us with God. I want to be a reflection of that. Amen.

THE BRIDGE TO OTHERS

*But now in Christ Jesus you who once were far away
have been brought near by the blood of Christ.*
EPHESIANS 2:13 NIV

If you look at the pop-up news articles on social media and see the distressing posts from your loved ones, it may seem like God is so far away from this world. You pray hard, but every day brings more challenges and another reason to never leave your house.

You should know that you're where you're at in life for a reason. With intentional love and actions, you do have the ability to affect the world around you. And that's exactly what Jesus wants us to do—bring people near to Him, just as you were brought close.

We have the chance to bridge the gaps between us and others, as a reflection of what Jesus has done for us. Is there anyone in your life you want to understand better? You can ask yourself how Jesus would approach them. You may just be the bridge your new friend needs to know Jesus.

---

*Jesus, how can I help be the bridge for
others to experience Your love?*

ATTITUDE

In your relationships with one another,
have the same mindset as Christ Jesus.
PHILIPPIANS 2:5 NIV

You've got a big test, so you focus *only* on your Bible-sized stack of index cards on the bus. You go to softball practice, and you know exactly what you need to work on. You spend two hours in the batting cage alone. You go home, so tired you zombie your way through dinner conversation with the family. Your dad asks you two times to pass the mashed potatoes!

What's wrong with this day? You got a lot done, that's for sure. But you never—not once—focused on the needs of someone else. You didn't think about what another might need. Someone on the bus was crying and needed someone to talk to. Your friend really wanted to practice her pitching. You could've practiced together. And your family just wanted to see your face!

Jesus offers us compassion, friendship, and comfort. When we take on the attitude of Christ, we start shifting our focus to others. We get the ability to see what they really need.

Jesus, I want Your attitude. I want to see
and fulfill what other people need.

HE IS FAITHFUL

God is faithful; you were called by him into
fellowship with his Son, Jesus Christ our Lord.
1 CORINTHIANS 1:9 CSB

When a fight in the friend group breaks out, you're the one who wants to bring peace. When your siblings argue, you're the one who suggests a compromise. You do all you can to keep everyone under control. But sooner or later, the people you thought you understood will surprise you. And maybe even hurt you.

Not everyone will do what you want them to, even when you believe you're right. Even if their actions hurt you, themselves, and others. But Jesus will never hurt you. He may do some surprising things, but it will always be for your benefit; you are always number one in His thoughts. Jesus is faithful. Not because of anything you've done or deserve but because He loves you unconditionally.

And this will never change. "Jesus Christ is the same yesterday and today and forever" (Hebrews 13:8 NLV).

Jesus, thank You for always being faithful and
consistent in my life. I can trust You!

TELL THEM

Jesus did not let him, but said, "Go home to your own people and tell them how much the Lord has done for you, and how he has had mercy on you."
MARK 5:19 NIV

Remember your first day of school? Not high school, but kindergarten. Did you run inside, excited, or did you cling to your parent's leg, so scared because of the new place and all the new faces?

Jesus healed a demon-possessed man, and this man wanted nothing more than to stay by Jesus' side. Who wouldn't? But Jesus had another plan for him. He wanted the man to go back home and tell everyone about what Jesus had done for him.

It can be so easy and way less scary to stay in our comfort zones and cling to Jesus and what He's done for us. But Jesus asks us, every day, to go out and share what we've got from Him with the entire world. And the good thing is you don't have to do it alone. Jesus won't leave your side. He is with you, every step of the way.

Jesus, show me where to tell others about what You've done. Amen.

A LIVING HOPE

*Because of his great mercy he has given. . .a living
hope through the resurrection of Jesus Christ
from the dead and into an inheritance that
is imperishable, undefiled, and unfading.*
1 PETER 1:3–4 CSB

There will be times in your life when everything feels shaky. Will
you get that scholarship? This essay will make or break it. You're
walking on eggshells around your friend. One word could dismantle
years of sleepovers and time spent together. You feel unsteady and
unsure; you have no idea where to place your next step.

We never have to worry about Jesus trembling. Not only is He
a hope for the future, He is a living hope. That means He is alive
right now and working out all things for your good (Romans 8:28).
Right now. He doesn't take breaks. No matter what happens with
the scholarship or your friend or whatever else you are dealing
with, you can trust that you have a future so wonderful and it
cannot be changed.

Jesus, no matter what happens, I trust You.

HAVE GREAT FAITH

"Woman, you have great faith! Your request is granted."
MATTHEW 15:28 NIV

We expect the mail to arrive at the same time every day. We expect summer to be hot and winter to be full of snow days. We expect the sun to rise each morning. There are so many things we expect to come through for us because that's what they've always done. But do you expect Jesus to do great things for you?

Jesus has already done so many good things for us so why is it so hard for us to trust that He will do it again? He wants us to expect great things from Him. He's Jesus!

When we are staring at the problem, sometimes the only thing we can see is the problem. But if we approach Jesus with the certainty and faith that He will help us tackle that issue, it is as good as done.

He will come through for you. Have great faith.

Jesus, I want to have great faith. I want to trust You. Amen.

HE IS RISEN!

"He has risen! He is not here."
MARK 16:6 NIV

You hear these words on Easter Sunday. They are written on flower wreaths and in stained glass windows. We sing them in hymns. They're words we see so often that we can easily forget the absolute magnificence of them. In our spiritual walk with the Lord, we can become so comfortable with this event that we hardly think about it.

Wonderfully, we know the end of the story, and if you grew up in the church, you've probably heard this story over and over again. But that shouldn't affect the way we view it.

Let's pretend as if we were hearing this story for the first time. Jesus, who was crucified, dead, and buried rose again. Those who visited the tomb were astounded. It was empty. Can you believe it? Nothing like this had ever happened before and hasn't happened since.

So whether it's Easter Sunday or the middle of winter, find a way to rejoice in the fact that He is risen! He conquered death and took away our sins!

Jesus, You are risen! Help me to always find amazement in that. Amen.

INTERRUPTIONS

So they got in the boat and went off to a remote
place by themselves. . . . When Jesus arrived, he
saw this huge crowd. At the sight of them, his
heart broke—like sheep with no shepherd they
were. He went right to work teaching them.
MARK 6:32, 34 MSG

You are so ready for some much-needed alone time. You've snuggled onto your couch with your favorite snack, ready to binge-watch that new show. But then your mom needs your help with the dishes. Your friend texts you with a problem she needs help solving. You see the elderly neighbor next door struggling with his trash.

Jesus and His disciples wanted some alone time. They even got on a boat to escape the crowds. But when Jesus saw that the people in the crowd needed something, He knew He was the only one who could help. He didn't hesitate.

When that happens to us, we have to ask Jesus for grace like His to help others without annoyance. We have to be able to let go of the plans we thought we wanted so that we can say "yes!" to even better ones.

Jesus, I ask for grace to help others when they need my help.

QUESTIONS

Jesus caught them off balance with his own test question: "What do you think about the Christ? Whose son is he?"

MATTHEW 22:41–42 MSG

Jesus came to make us look differently at the world. To make us question ideas and thoughts and rules we wouldn't normally question. He wants people to really think about what they believe and why. Jesus had trick questions for everyone: the religious leaders, His disciples, and strangers. So you know He has some questions for you.

Do you think you know what some of those questions should be? Take some quiet time to really listen to Jesus and what He has to say. When you do, Jesus will reveal ways of looking at scripture, others, and the world that you may never have thought of before. Don't be scared. Even when you feel shaken, Jesus will be there to remind you to find stability in Him. You're growing your faith. You are exactly where you need to be.

Okay, Jesus, I'm listening. What questions do You have for me?

INSTANT MESSENGER

You show that you are Christ's letter. . .not written with ink but with the Spirit of the living God—not on tablets of stone but on tablets of human hearts.
2 CORINTHIANS 3:3 CSB

When the internet was new, there was a type of messenger your parents probably used. You came up with a screen name to chat with your friends. You could connect with someone you'd never met before or catch up with a friend who had moved away. It was the first time people could talk to one another over the internet in real time.

Did you know that Jesus sent you a message? And He wrote it as a way to connect with us when He went away. He left the Holy Spirit behind, who wrote Jesus' promises on our hearts. If you've accepted Jesus, you can be in constant conversation with Him. You not only have the chance to speak with Him, but you can be a way that others know Him because you act the way Jesus wants you to.

Jesus, thanks for the message! Help me to show You the best way I can.

HIS COMFORT

For just as we share abundantly in the sufferings of Christ, so also our comfort abounds through Christ.
2 Corinthians 1:5 niv

Jesus promises to comfort you in every tough moment of your life—during a fight with a friend, the death of a loved one, a disappointing outcome to a college application, or a school tryout, and during the loneliness you just can't escape on certain days. Why? Because Jesus knows what it was like to suffer. He knows about pain and heartache. Jesus shares in your sufferings, but because He understands our sufferings, He knows what will bring us boundless comfort.

This comfort He offers tells you that you are not alone and that this hard moment is temporary. And He's right there with you through it all. Just reach out to Him today.

Jesus, I need Your comfort. I need You. I know You have suffered greatly, and I know that I will suffer too. But I will also find rest in Your truth that You will always extend what I need to get through.

YOU DON'T HAVE TO TRY SO HARD

*If we could be made right with God by keeping
the Law, then Christ died for nothing.*
GALATIANS 2:21 NLV

You volunteer for every mission trip, memorize every key scripture your small-group mentor tells you to, and are the first in a pew on Sunday morning...because that proves you're a good Christian. You feel as if you have to earn Jesus' sacrifice and His love.

Jesus wouldn't agree with that. If we could save ourselves with good works, then, as Paul wrote, Jesus would have died for nothing. While Jesus wants you to do good works, He doesn't want you doing them because they get you to heaven but because you love Him. And because you want to love others. You never have to prove yourself worthy of His love—you're already loved!

The gospel isn't about what you can do. It's about what Jesus has done for you. So breathe. You don't have to try so hard. Jesus has got you!

---

*Thank You, Jesus, that I don't have to work for Your
love. I want to do good because I love You!*

ALL-NIGHTER

Get your minds ready for good use. Keep awake.
Set your hope now and forever on the loving-favor
to be given you when Jesus Christ comes again.
1 PETER 1:13 NLV

If you go to college, chances are you are going to spend some time chugging coffee in front of a screen to finish a paper that is due at seven the next morning, and it's ten o'clock at night when you sit down to write the first word. You're pulling an all-nighter!

Jesus asks us to pull an all-nighter too. We live in a dark world. We have a hope in Him that He will come and rescue this world from this all-consuming night. We have to be vigilant for this time, continuing His legacy of kindness and love on earth as we follow Him. Get your mind ready by spending time in His Word and in His presence. Stay awake, and do not fall into the hate and negativity this world creates. Wait for Him; He will not disappoint.

Jesus, I will stay awake!

BELIEVE

"Repent and believe the good news!"
MARK 1:15 CSB

How many times have you prayed "The Sinner's Prayer"? Every time a worship leader or a pastor asks the congregation if they've accepted Jesus into their hearts, do you bow your head and ask Jesus again, just in case the last time didn't work? Our humanness makes it hard to trust a lot of things. Unfortunately, that means we may have a hard time believing that Jesus really did die for our sins, and we question if our prayer really worked.

You don't have to keep re-saving yourself every day. Jesus has promised you grace when you call on Him and change your ways. It only takes one prayer, and then there is nothing you can do for Him to take away His vow. You're His beloved, His reason; His love for you is never-ending. Do you believe that?

Sit with Him today and tell Him your sins, and believe that He has saved you.

Jesus, I want to tell You this today: I believe that You have saved me. Amen.

REPENTANCE

*"I have not come to call the righteous,
but sinners to repentance."*
Luke 5:32 csb

Repentance can be a scary word. If you don't do it, you're told scary things will happen. Repentance, when looked at through human eyes, tells us that the only things we can ever be are terrible, sin-filled people. Jesus had no intention of making His beloved feel like that. So when we look at repentance in the way Jesus did, it can show us that we were just meant for so much more than this world.

Jesus' idea of repentance gives you hope and joy and tells your fears and failures to hit the road. It reconnects you with your heavenly Father. It says that you are not the mistakes you've made but the wonderful creation made new in Jesus Christ. Jesus doesn't point fingers, pass blame, or make you feel ashamed. You can repent bravely, knowing you're deeply loved by Jesus and He wants you to be saved.

---

*Jesus, I come to You unashamed in
repentance. I trust that You saved me.*

A GREAT LIFE

"I came so they might have life, a great full life."
JOHN 10:10 NLV

Some days are just good days. Maybe you love a sunny day in the summer and you spend as much time as you can outside by the pool or in the park. Maybe you love rainy springs and curling up with a good book by an open window. Autumn can bring beautiful colors, comfy sweaters, and spooky movies. And a winter snow day can bring rest and comfort and time with family.

When we are going through a hard month, one good day can do a lot. . .like remind us that we were never meant for this world, this hurt, this longing.

Jesus wants all our days to be really good days. That's why He came. To give us not only life but a great and full life. While we face hard times on earth, those glimpses of goodness in between remind us of the life we will experience with and because of Jesus Christ.

Jesus, thank You for the good days and the good life. Amen!

INSECURITY

That is why, for Christ's sake, I delight in weaknesses, in insults, in hardships, in persecutions, in difficulties. For when I am weak, then I am strong.
2 CORINTHIANS 12:10 NIV

Insecurity is that really gross thought of not feeling good enough. We can be insecure about the grades we get in school, about what our friends or crushes think of us, and about the way we look, act, and feel. Insecurity comes when we see expectations and we compare ourselves to how others are meeting those expectations.

But those expectations are not from Jesus, they were created by the world. Jesus doesn't care one wink about the world's expectations. He spent most of His life on earth defying those expectations anyway. And we are supposed to be like Him!

When our insecurity comes because we've failed to meet expectations, we can actually rejoice in that. Because Jesus wants us to rely on Him when we feel lost, alone, and weak. He can use insecurity as a reminder that you can find wholeness and perfection only in Him.

Jesus, when I feel insecure, I will go to You.

PERFECT

"You must be perfect as your
Father in heaven is perfect."
MATTHEW 5:48 NLV

This verse may make you cringe. And it seems almost impossible. How could we ever match up to the perfection of our Father in heaven? Thank goodness that we know someone who did just that—lived a life as perfect as God's. Jesus lived this life and then gave it up on the cross. So we didn't have to.

He saved us from a life of trying so hard to walk the tightrope of perfection and falling off every couple of steps. With His forgiveness, our sins are taken care of. With His grace, we can be free from the expectations of being the "perfect Christian girl." You are free to be the best version of you without stumbling over your own, world-sized view of perfection.

Jesus, what was it like to be perfect? I'll never know, but
I don't care. Thank You that I don't have to work so hard
or make myself feel bad when I don't quite make it.

A PROMISE OF ETERNITY

Blessed is the one who perseveres under trial
because, having stood the test, that person
will receive the crown of life that the Lord
has promised to those who love him.
JAMES 1:12 NIV

This verse is a lot like the ones Jesus said in the Beatitudes. (Check out Matthew 5 for those!) The writer of this passage explains that we can consider it a blessing when we have the chance to say no to temptations. Because when we do, we can know that Jesus has made us a promise that says if we try our best, always choosing Him first, we get a whole eternity with Him. That's way better than any temporary pleasure this world offers.

Why would He do this and why would we want to? Because He loves us, and we love Him. This world may count us as weak, but we're strong in Him. And when you need help to overcome temptation, you can rely on His strength to get through.

Jesus, thank You for this promise of eternity. As I go through a hard season, I know there is light at the end of it. I can press on.

EVERYTHING NEW

Then the one seated on the throne said,
"Look, I am making everything new."
REVELATION 21:5 CSB

You are a part of one beautiful story. A story of love that begins in the creation of the world in Genesis and ends in the promise of Jesus' return in Revelation. The day you were born and took your first breath, your life added meaning to this story. Your days became the pages; new times in life brought chapters that switched genres from children's to young adult. And by grace, your story will continue.

And Jesus has already worked out the ending—forever with Him. For when you call on Jesus and want to walk in His ways, it's not the ending but the beginning. He makes all things new. You don't have to live in the old ways anymore.

Your story is one of trial and of tribulation. It is of suffering but also of rescue. It is of hardship and forgiveness. All in the name of Jesus, your Savior, who is always making new things—making you a new thing.

Jesus, thank You for the promise of making everything new. Amen.

IN SICKNESS AND IN HEALTH

Yet he himself bore our sicknesses,
and he carried our pains.
ISAIAH 53:4 CSB

If you've ever been to a wedding, you've probably heard the couple recite that they will love one another in sickness and in health. And something we learn the hard way is. . .there are a lot of times of sickness in this world. Colds. The flu. Broken bones. Cancer. The human body goes through a lot.

Jesus knew this. . .and willingly gave up His divine body—that could never get sick or hurt—and took His place in humanity as one of us. Truly one of us. He knows what it's like to get sick. He knows what it's like to feel pain.

Jesus endured real sickness and physical hurt to ultimately heal our spiritual pain. Whether we are in sickness or in health, He still saves us from sin and this world.

Jesus, I can't believe You would do that for me. Being sick is never fun. Thank You, Jesus, that I can look forward to a time of no pain or sickness.

THE SERMON ON THE MOUNT

When he saw the crowds, he went up on the mountain, and after he sat down, his disciples came to him. Then he began to teach them, saying. . .
MATTHEW 5:1–2 CSB

Imagine you were there that day: The heat of the sun and the mountain breeze on your face. The soft but powerful voice of Jesus giving one of the most important sermons of all time. He starts with the powerful promise that you're blessed when you go through trials, because you'll be rewarded in heaven. He reminds believers that they're the salt and light of the earth, the ones who should be making it a better place. He declares that He's the one to fulfill the law the prophets spoke of. He says to not hate, murder, or cheat, and to always tell the truth, to always try your best at everything you do, and so much more.

But everything really boils down to the core idea that will make you want to follow and believe everything listed above: Love! You must love one another. That's why Jesus came. To show the world how love really acts.

Jesus, how can I show love today for others?

YOUR WORDS ARE POWERFUL

When he got to the tree, there was nothing but fig
leaves. He said, "No more figs from this tree—ever!"
The fig tree withered on the spot, a dry stick.
MATTHEW 21:19 MSG

You say something about yourself that you would never say about your best friend. You tell yourself over and over again there is no way you will get that grade, ace that audition, join the team. For the last couple of days, negativity is the only thing coming out of your mouth, and it feels like a storm cloud is following you around.

We see an image of Jesus in Scripture, doing something pretty crazy—talking to a tree and making it wilt. Even the disciples had no idea why Jesus did this. Was He really just hangry? Enough to curse an entire tree?

Maybe Jesus was trying to show us that our words are powerful. They have the power to encourage and to destroy. So we need to use our words wisely—especially when we talk to ourselves. Use your words as positive encouragement instead of negativity.

Jesus, I want to be positive! I will watch my words.

JESUS' DEATH

Jesus called out with a loud voice, "Father,
into your hands I commit my spirit." When
he had said this, he breathed his last.

LUKE 23:46 NIV

Jesus died. He went through hours of severe and painful torture before He was taken to the cross. He was humiliated and shamed. He spent His last moments completely alone. We call the day Jesus died Good Friday, but there was really nothing good about it. Our Savior was given a punishment He didn't deserve.

We can sometimes gloss over this day as we head straight to Sunday morning—to the glorious moment Jesus rose—but there's also glory in the moment He died, the moment He gave up His divinity, His life, for us. This was not only an act of amazing love; it was a display of ultimate power. Because what is more powerful than choosing to give up that power for the benefit of someone you love.

Sit with that thought today, alongside the living Jesus, and see what He reveals to you.

Jesus, thank You for what You did for me on the cross. Amen.

BEING A LEADER

*Don't let anyone look down on you because you
are young, but set an example for the believers in
speech, in conduct, in love, in faith and in purity.*
1 TIMOTHY 4:12 NIV

"You're just a kid. You'll get it when you're older. You don't know
how good you have it." How infuriating it is to be told that! Being
young doesn't mean your struggles aren't real or that you don't
have to deal with serious, difficult issues.

Guess what? Jesus doesn't believe that. He believes that you
have your own life with your own problems and that you are called
to shine through those issues just like everyone else. Timothy was
young and still used by Jesus. You can be too.

In fact, Jesus goes beyond that. You are called to lead! Show the
"adults" how you are supposed to love people, and be the leader
some might say that you can't be.

---

*Jesus, please help me keep my cool when people belittle
my age. Show me how to love everyone better through it.*

HE IS PRESENT

*"I am the Alpha and the Omega, the first
and the last, the beginning and the end."*

REVELATION 22:13 CSB

Jesus is your Savior. He's your best friend and your confidant. He is the King of Kings, the Prince of Peace. He is a redeemer and a comforter. He is nature in its most beautiful form. He is the light that drives out darkness. He is goodness and love. He is so many things, and most of all, Jesus is present.

Jesus isn't a ruler who looks down from his throne in the sky. He hasn't left the world or you behind. He is actively working to continue His legacy of saving this world. He's not an absent parent or a long-lost relative. Jesus longs for connection with you. You may not be able to see Him, and some days you may not be able to even feel Him, but He never left you.

Make a list of things that Jesus means to you. What are some times in your life you knew Jesus came through for you?

_____

Jesus, this is what You mean to me. . .

JESUS' BAPTISM

But Jesus insisted. "Do it. God's work, putting things right all these centuries, is coming together right now in this baptism." So John did it.

MATTHEW 3:15 MSG

Have you ever been baptized? It is a declaration that you decided to follow Jesus. It's also a representation of the physical act of what happens when we ask Jesus for forgiveness. We're plunged into the depths, sometimes the unknown, and we come out a different person, clean from our past and our sins.

Jesus' ministry on earth began with His baptism. He didn't need to do this, because He was sinless. John the Baptist even said that Jesus should be the one baptizing him (Matthew 3:14). But by doing so, Jesus showed the world that He truly was the Son of God. God even said so from the heavens (Matthew 3:17)!

At this moment, Jesus knew the hardships He would endure, but He also knew how the story would end. In a triumphant victory over sin and death. We can rejoice in that today too!

Jesus! You are the Son of God, and I rejoice in that today!

WAITING

"You don't have to wait for the End. I am, right now, Resurrection and Life. The one who believes in me, even though he or she dies, will live. And everyone who lives believing in me does not ultimately die at all. Do you believe this?"

JOHN 11:25–26 MSG

Waiting. Right now, it may feel like all you do is wait. For the bus, for your paycheck, for your brother to pick you up, for your crush to ask you to the dance. In your faith, you may feel like you're waiting a lot on Jesus. You're waiting for healing, for comfort, for opportunities to come your way, and for the time He returns.

But Jesus wants you to know that you don't have to wait for eternity. That time actually starts the moment you ask Him into your heart. You started living with forever in mind at that moment, and spiritually, you will never die. Jesus asks, "Do you believe this?" As you wait on future blessings, you can rest in comfort of this already fulfilled promise.

Jesus, I believe that I don't have to wait for Your forgiveness and life. I have it right now!

KNOW JESUS, KNOW GOD.

"If you had known Me, you would know My Father also. From now on you know Him and have seen Him."
John 14:7 NLV

If you know Jesus, you know God. A disciple named Philip had a hard time understanding this concept. He even asked Jesus to show him the Father. But Jesus explained that Jesus was the Father, and Jesus was doing His work. Philip had the chance to know God because he knew Jesus.

It can be confusing, but it's still the same for us today. We have a relationship with God because we have a relationship with Jesus. They're one and the same. Jesus died for our sins, tore the veil that separated humanity and God. And if we believe that, Jesus says, "whoever believes in me will do the works I have been doing, and they will do even greater things than these" (John 14:12 NIV). We've been given the power to extend kindness, make the world a better place because of this love first extended to us.

Jesus, it's confusing, but I trust I'm known and accepted by God because I'm known and accepted by You.

FAITH EXPRESSED IN LOVE!

When you attempt to live by your own religious plans and projects, you are cut off from Christ, you fall out of grace. Meanwhile we expectantly wait for a satisfying relationship with the Spirit. For in Christ, neither our most conscientious religion nor disregard of religion amounts to anything. What matters is something far more interior: faith expressed in love.

GALATIANS 5:4–6 MSG

Jesus loves you and accepts you completely. It doesn't matter what you have done. It actually doesn't matter what you do. You don't have to change your wardrobe, attend ten Bible studies, join the worship team or a new church, or "fix" the way you speak or act. You are saved by Jesus, the moment you put your faith in Him. But as His Spirit truly works in your heart, you start wanting to act in love—love for yourself and for others. And that's what Jesus thinks is most important: when your faith in Him is expressed fully in acts of love. What are some ways you can express your faith in love today?

_____

Jesus, I know I want a "faith expressed in love." What can I do?

COME ALIVE

Death initially came by a man, and resurrection
from death came by a man. Everybody dies in
Adam; everybody comes alive in Christ.
1 CORINTHIANS 15:21–22 MSG

Those long days that lead to even longer nights that feel as if they'll never end. . . You wake up and go through the motions, but you're finding it hard to find motivation, to dream, to be thankful. Joy is gone and has been replaced with something that has the power to kill—apathy. You've stopped caring.

But stop for a moment and listen. Can you hear it? Jesus is asking you to come alive. He wants you to care about your life, about the big events and the little moments. This transition out of apathy won't be easy; it won't happen overnight, and you may need to seek more help from those you trust. You may need to attend therapy or programs or use certain medications that were created to help.

But Jesus will be with you. You're alive in Christ, just by having faith in Him. He wants you to be able to enjoy that.

Jesus, I confess I've stopped caring. Show me how to start again.

NEVER FOR HIS OWN BENEFIT

*In your relationships with one another, have the
same mindset as Christ Jesus: Who, being in very
nature God, did not consider equality with God
something to be used to his own advantage.*

PHILIPPIANS 2:5–6 NIV

Ever make a choice purely for another's benefit? Whether an easy
or hard choice, in the end, you knew it was the best choice because
you acted out of love.

Jesus was a selfless person. He was constantly thinking about
who needed His help. And for most of His life, Jesus used His power
from God to help. But He never ever used His divine power for
His own benefit.

In the desert when He was tempted to use His powers, He never
did (Matthew 4:1–11). On the cross, He was told to save Himself
(Luke 23:37). He certainly had the power to do so but chose not
to. Because He needed to die to save us.

He always used His divine powers for our benefit, never His own.

---

*Jesus, thank You for loving us so much that You only used
Your power for me. Help me to benefit others the way You do.*

PEACE DURING A PROBLEM

Let the peace of Christ rule in your hearts,
since as members of one body you were
called to peace. And be thankful.
COLOSSIANS 3:15 NIV

This problem just—won't—go—away. No matter what you do, like a pesky math equation you can't seem to figure out, you're stuck in it. But it's way worse than a math problem. And unfortunately, you know that you'll need to solve it sometime. But you have no idea how!

It can be easy to get frustrated. It can be even easier to lose hope. But when we accept Jesus into our hearts, we are granted peace that should rule over our hearts. When we take this problem to Jesus, that is when we can find this peace. When we stop trying to fix it all on our own, that's when we open ourselves up to comfort. Peace can renew strength, rebuild hope, and offer time to figure it all out.

And maybe in this peace and stillness, you find a way to solve the problem.

Jesus, help me to focus on peace instead of my problem.

IN THE MIDST OF EVERYTHING

In everything give thanks. This is what God
wants you to do because of Christ Jesus.
1 Thessalonians 5:18 nlv

How do you possibly give thanks in times of hardship, trouble, or heartache? How do you even want to? When you have pain or disappointment, do you thank God for those things? Maybe in the future you will, but in the moment, Jesus isn't asking you to give thanks *for* something but *in* the midst of something. In the midst of everything, give thanks.

Jesus has a way of reminding us of blessings, of what we can still be thankful for when our lives feel out of control. This is His will. Because when you thank Him in the middle of a trial, it shows that you trust Him above all things—above doubts and feelings, above life's circumstances. You trust Him to come through for you, even if you cannot see Him or feel Him working.

When negative thoughts start to overtake you, start making a list of things you're thankful for. You may find some comfort.

Jesus, show me what it means to be thankful
in the midst of absolutely everything.

A PLACE TO BELONG

"My Father's house has many rooms; if that were not so, would I have told you that I am going there to prepare a place for you? And if I go and prepare a place for you, I will come back and take you to be with me that you also may be where I am."

JOHN 14:2–3 NIV

Do you battle with loneliness? It's more than having no one to sit with at lunch or being left out. It's that creeping feeling you get when you lie in bed at night that says no one likes you. It's that drone of dread, realizing you're in a room full of people and no one is listening. It's believing you'll never be understood.

Those feelings are really hard. But thankfully, you do have a place to belong. With Jesus. He tells us that we always have a place with Him. It can mean your home for eternity, but it also means that today—right now—He is offering a place of comfort, of peace, of friendship, and of complete understanding. You just have to go to Him.

Jesus, I am lonely. I come to You today, knowing You understand.

133

PROTECTED

"I give them eternal life, and they will never perish.
No one will snatch them out of my hand."
JOHN 10:28 CSB

Once you've given your life to Jesus, you're granted the gift of life with Him in heaven. No one knows what that will be like until it happens to them, but we know it will be glorious. And unlike so many things of this world, nothing and no one can take that away from you. That promise is protected. And so are you. He's holding on with a fierce, loving hold. He's not letting you go, and He won't let His promises be taken away from you.

Anything that you've done, anything someone has done to you will never diminish Jesus' love or His promises. You can breathe freely in this truth. This world does awful things, and sometimes we don't know why. Jesus grieves with us and urges us to rejoice that there will be a day when all is well again. No pain and no brokenness.

Your future is protected in Jesus.

Jesus, thank You for holding on to me. I'll try to live in the truth that eternal life will never be taken away from me.

TREASURE

"For where your treasure is,
there your heart will be also."
MATTHEW 6:21 NIV

You may have a lot of things that you consider treasure: the gold necklace that belonged to your great-grandmother, the money you saved up working at that summer camp, the car your parents got you for your birthday, the way you look. Sometimes treasure can be things you do—like getting grades or using your talents.

We can get so caught up in the things of this world that we start placing our heart with those things. That means we rely on them to make us feel happy or fulfilled, to give us self-esteem or worth. Unfortunately, we are setting ourselves up for heartache if we do that. Because everything in this world will come to an end (Matthew 6:19).

Jesus never ends. He's forever. If we place our heart in Him, we place it with everlasting love and immeasurable worth. We'll never be disappointed or let down. That's where our treasure should be!

Jesus, open my eyes to where my treasure is. Amen.

FOREVER AND EVER!

"I am the Living One; I was dead, and now look, I am alive for ever and ever!"
REVELATION 1:18 NIV

The actual driving portion of your driver's test went great! But when it comes to maneuverability, you knock over one orange traffic cone. That means you have to take this part of the test again to get it right so you can finally get your license.

Sometimes in life we have to do things over again to get them right. We don't have to worry about that with what Jesus has done for us. He never has to make the sacrifice He made on the cross again. His one death vanquished death for us forever; His sacrifice covers all sin for all time. Hebrews 9:26 (CSB) says, "Otherwise, he would have had to suffer many times since the foundation of the world. But now he has appeared one time, at the end of the ages, for the removal of sin by the sacrifice of himself." He never has to die again. He'll stay alive forever and ever!

Jesus, I believe that what You did covers all my sins for all time. Thank You!

NEVER SEPARATED

But Jesus cried out again with a loud voice and gave up his spirit. Suddenly, the curtain of the sanctuary was torn in two from top to bottom, the earth quaked, and the rocks were split.

MATTHEW 27:50–51 CSB

When we have to be separated from our friends or family members, it can be painful. We love them and we want to be with them! Before Jesus came, God's people were separated from Him because of this broken world and sin. This hurt God so much to be separated from His creation in this way. He missed us so much!

But Jesus changed all that. In the moment He gave up His spirit on the cross, the curtain of the sanctuary that once kept people out of God's presence was ripped apart. This was to show that sin that had once separated us from God was taken care of. We can now enjoy being with our Savior every single day, all the time. We will never be separated from Him.

Thank You, Jesus, for the truth that I never will be separated from Your love.

BUT SEE JESUS

But we do see Jesus.
HEBREWS 2:9 NLV

A college girl, lost in loneliness, found herself in front of a photograph of strange-looking shadowy trees. Faint light filtered through the branches, but it was still dark. Just like how she felt on the inside. She fell to her knees in front of the artwork. She was so done with feeling so sad. And through her tears, she looked up. Those trees weren't twisted; they made the shape of the cross, right where the light shone through.

When we look at what happens in this world, it can be easy to see only pride and pain, disappointment and loneliness, and so much suffering. But we can also see Jesus if we change our perspective. He is in the speck of kindness between strangers, in the time spent with loved ones. He is in an aspect of nature or in a piece of art that moves us emotionally. Choose to see Him in your everyday life and find joy that He is present.

Jesus, I want to see You more. Open my eyes to You.

A NEW LIFE

For if a man belongs to Christ, he is a new person.
The old life is gone. New life has begun.
2 CORINTHIANS 5:17 NLV

Every single day you are reminded of who you were before you truly knew Jesus. And to be honest, you don't really like that person. Maybe you didn't know Jesus at all. Maybe you knew of Him but used religion as your weapon. Either way, you hurt others. The scars left on your life from pain that happened to you or from the pain you caused others can be so visible if we are constantly looking at them through a lens of guilt.

You have a brand-new life in Christ. We should seek forgiveness for the wrong things we've done, but we don't have to live in shame or continually punish ourselves. A new life has started. We can create new, healthy boundaries for ourselves and others. We can make choices out of love for others and for ourselves. We are no longer stuck in the past because Jesus has set us free!

Jesus, thank You for this new life. Amen.

⌐ HIS YOKE ⌐

"Take my yoke upon you and learn from me, for I am gentle and humble in heart, and you will find rest for your souls. For my yoke is easy and my burden is light."
MATTHEW 11:29–30 NIV

A yoke is a piece of wood that lies over the shoulders of two animals to allow them to pull a heavy cart. In life, we get our own yoke that helps us carry our life's problems. Some days, it feels as if your cart is basically empty. And the yoke is light on your back. But some days, the cart is full and heavy and the yoke is digging into your skin.

On those days, we keep trying to pull that cart full of our problems, even though we're exhausted. Jesus is waiting to trade our yoke for His. He is gentle and humble. He never asks us to carry more than we can without His help. When you allow Jesus to help you pull those burdens, you can find actual rest.

Jesus, I want Your yoke and to find true rest.
I'm sorry for always trying to do it on my own.

YOU CAN DO IT!

I can do all this through him who gives me strength.
PHILIPPIANS 4:13 NIV

You've been staring at the sign-up sheet for weeks. You've been thinking about that deadline quickly approaching every moment of the day. You want this more than anything. But there is that little voice in your head that says you can't do it. It says you'll never be enough.

Guess what? That's not true. You can do it. And you can rely on Jesus for strength, courage, and comfort to do it. You can do anything with Jesus by your side.

You already know this doesn't mean that you'll always be successful. And that will hurt. But Jesus will be with you in those moments too, with peace and an assurance that you will be able to try again or choose to move on.

The Message version of Philippians 4:13 says it best: "Whatever I have, wherever I am, I can make it through anything in the One who makes me who I am." Say it loud: "I can do it!"

Jesus, I can do it!

141

PERFECT?

*"Martha, Martha, you are worried and
upset about many things, but one thing is
necessary. Mary has made the right choice,
and it will not be taken away from her."*
LUKE 10:41–42 CSB

Social media tells us we need to have the perfect body. That one teacher always makes you feel like you have to get perfect grades. Your grandparents expect you to be the perfect version of the granddaughter they want. When you look at these expectations, you could have a meltdown! You just want to be you.

Jesus shows in this story that you don't have to be perfect for Him to be a part of your life. Martha was having a meltdown that her house wasn't perfect for Jesus, and her sister, Mary, wasn't helping at all. But Jesus assured Martha that Mary was doing the right thing just by sitting in His presence. She didn't have to make everything perfect for Him first. And He says the same to us. The world's expectations can wait. Just go to Jesus as you are.

---

*Jesus, I am so glad I don't have to be perfect
to be loved by You. Thanks!*

COMMANDED TO LOVE

"Go, therefore, and make disciples. . .teaching them to observe everything I have commanded you."
MATTHEW 28:19–20 CSB

Before Jesus went to heaven, He told His followers to continue teaching others about what He commanded them. *Commanded* is a strong word. It's more than telling. It's more than a suggestion. If a parent uses that certain voice and commands you to apologize to your sibling, you know you better do it. Jesus commanded something. So what did He command?

"Love one another" (John 13:34 NIV). Jesus commands us to love. And He commands us to command others to love as well. And sometimes just the act of loving is enough to get someone else to love in their own way. Hopefully, that leads to a lot of love going around.

When loving someone is hard or nerve-racking, Jesus tells you, "Remember, I am with you always, to the end of the age" (Matthew 28:20 CSB). You don't have to do it alone. Jesus will help you and show you the right way to love someone.

Jesus, help me to see how and when I can show love!

HOW TO PRAY

He said to them, "When you pray, say..."
LUKE 11:2 NIV

Praying can be hard. You hear these long, eloquent prayers at church and wonder if the Lord is really listening to little ole you. You may fold your hands and close your eyes and find yourself suddenly speechless. Or maybe at night, in bed, you fall asleep before you get to "Amen." God loves to hear from you, no matter what, but Jesus created a prayer that helps us speak when we don't know what to say.

"Father, hallowed be your name, your kingdom come" (Luke 11:2 NIV). You can start by declaring that God is near. You know He is.

"Give us each day our daily bread" (verse 3). Ask God to provide for your needs.

"Forgive us our sins, for we also forgive everyone who sins against us" (verse 4). Seek forgiveness but also seek the courage, humility, and kindness to forgive others.

"And lead us not into temptation" (verse 4). Ask for the strength to stay away from sin.

Jesus finishes by saying that God wants to hear from you. You just have to start talking.

Jesus, I want to try and pray like You did.

LET IT SHINE!

"Keep your eyes open, your lamp burning, so you don't get musty and murky. Keep your life as well-lighted as your best-lighted room."
LUKE 11:35–36 MSG

Come on, you know the song! "This little light of mine, I'm gonna let it shine!" You learn this song when you're really little about sharing the light of Jesus with others, but it can also describe letting Jesus' light transform your entire being.

We all have dark parts of ourselves that we hide from the world. But we can't hide them from Jesus. He knows all about the things we keep in the dark—and that's a good thing. Because He wants you to let His light shine, clear away the cobwebs and dust and shame to reveal who you're really supposed to be.

When you let Jesus light up your entire life, that's when you don't even have to try to share His light with others. It just happens.

Jesus, let it shine! I am so done with shame and darkness. I want to live like I was meant to!

LAZARUS RAISED

"I am the resurrection and the life. The one who believes in me will live, even though they die."
JOHN 11:25 NIV

Jesus made YOU a promise. If you believe in Him, you'll have eternal life with Him. No one knows what that looks like. Well, maybe one person. . .

Mary and Martha had lost their brother. He had been dead four days when Jesus finally arrived. Of course they were upset. They knew Jesus had the power to heal him, but they thought it was too late. However, Jesus knew that He could use this tragedy to show the sisters and everyone else that He had power over death. Even though it looked bleak and impossible, Jesus asked them to still have faith in Him.

And being the absolute resurrection and life, Jesus raised Lazarus from the dead. Just as He did Himself, three days after paying the price of the world's sins.

We may experience physical death here on earth, but we will never have to go through spiritual death, because of what Jesus has done.

---

*Jesus, thank You so much. I don't have to
fear what happens after I die.*

OBEY IT

*"Blessed rather are those who hear
the word of God and obey it."*
LUKE 11:28 NIV

This may be a hard thing for you to read. Going to church every Sunday doesn't make you a good person. Reading the Bible every day doesn't make you a good person. Saying you're a Christian doesn't make you a good person.

Jesus knew that our actions as His followers would speak so much louder than our words ever could. So He tells the crowds that want to know more about Him and live in His life that the ones who will actually be blessed are the ones who not only hear what He says. . .but the ones who actually do it.

Some people may have grumbled because they thought Jesus was supposed to make it easier to get to their heavenly reward. They turned and left. But we know there were others who let their hearts be changed and decided that they truly wanted to love people. Not only say they did.

Jesus' teachings are meant to be followed. Obey. He knew what He was talking about.

---

*Jesus, I want to follow Your teachings and
be who You meant me to be.*

NEVER BURDEN

"Woe to you, because you load people down
with burdens they can hardly carry, and you
yourselves will not lift one finger to help them."
LUKE 11:46 NIV

When Jesus was on earth, the church of that time had a lot of rules. Jesus warned the leaders of religion at the time that they were actually keeping people away from a relationship with God because of all the rules they created. They wouldn't lift a finger to help anyone who needed help following God. When they themselves weren't following most of His commandments anyway!

Modern-day churches and modern-day Christ followers sometimes do that too. Whether they mean to or not. Jesus tells us everyone is acceptable and worthy of God's love. We were never supposed to burden others with a long list of everything they've done and what they have to do. We were never meant to watch others struggle aimlessly with shame and guilt without helping.

Jesus loves every person you come in contact with. He wants you to love them too.

Jesus, I don't want to keep anyone from knowing
You. How can I love and help people?

KEEP ON GOING IN YOUR CALLING

We can only keep on going, after all, by the power of God, who first saved us and then called us to this holy work. . . . It was all his idea, a gift prepared for us in Jesus long before we knew anything about it

2 Timothy 1:9 MSG

We're called to love others and to introduce them to Jesus. The gift in this—prepared for us by Jesus before we're even born—is that you have a very special thing that lets you love others in the way only you can. You have the story, the talent, or the personality that cares for others in just the right way.

When we find this part of our calling, we have to remember to keep the focus on Jesus. When we rely too much on ourselves, things like insecurity and pride can get in our way. Whether you're still figuring it out or have found it years ago, remember to always radiate confidence that reflects your Savior when you're loving others by doing what you love.

Jesus, I will keep on going in this calling of loving others and showing them You. Amen.

HE NEVER GIVES UP

"I stand at the door and knock. If anyone hears my voice and opens the door, I will come in."
REVELATION 3:20 NIV

You finally finished. Your first 5K marathon. Your final college scholarship essay. Your audition for first chair in orchestra. When you finish something you've been working hard on for soooo long, you'll look back at the times you wanted to give up, and you'll be so glad you didn't. Because you never would've experienced the amazing feelings of humble pride and accomplishment.

Jesus is in pursuit after you. Except He never once thinks about quitting. Jesus wants to have a relationship with you. He stands at the door of your heart and knocks, unrelenting. The moment you open the door, He never hesitates. He enters and is a part of your life.

In this world, people may choose to leave you. They may give up on you. Not Jesus. He won't ever give you up. He will keep chasing after you until you ask Him into your heart and your life.

Jesus, I heard Your knocking. I want You to be a part of my life.

JESUS' COAT

The soldiers who nailed Jesus to the cross took
His clothes and divided them in four parts, each
soldier getting one part. But His coat which
was not sewed was made in one piece.
JOHN 19:23 NLV

This is one part of the cross that we sometimes gloss over: Jesus' coat. We have no idea what that may have looked like (it was actually more of an undergarment than a cloak or cape), but some people associate the color purple with it, because in Bible times, purple was usually associated with royalty. And even amid His pain and the mocking, Jesus still had the dignity of the King of Kings.

"Then Pilate put a writing on the cross which said, JESUS OF NAZARETH, THE KING OF THE JEWS" (John 19:19 NLV). This was created to actually put Jesus to shame, but in reality, Pilate was writing the truth. Jesus is the King. And He still rules today.

Jesus, I know that You're the King of Kings. Thank
You for scripture that reminds me of that.

THE KING!

He is the head over all the kings of the earth.
REVELATION 1:5 NLV

Do you like being in charge? Maybe you're the president of your 4-H club, captain of your cheer squad, or the leader for your science project. It can be fun to be in charge! But you know that with a place of leadership comes a lot of responsibility. You have to make all the decisions, and everyone is looking to you for what to do next.

Sometimes we fail at being good leaders. Kings have to rule entire countries, and even they mess up. Thank goodness, we have a perfect leader to follow. Jesus said, "My kingdom is not of this world. . . . My kingdom is from another place. . . . You say that I am a king. In fact, the reason I was born and came into the world is to testify to the truth" (John 18:36–37 NIV). He is the King of Kings and ruler of the world. He was always meant to be. And we can trust Him.

Jesus, You are the King! I can trust Your rule in my life. Amen!

MARKED ON HIS HANDS

"I will not forget you. See, I have marked
your names on My hands."
ISAIAH 49:15–16 NLV

Forgotten. Left out. Unnoticed. These are a few words that we really don't want to be associated with. You want to be remembered, included, and noticed. But in this imperfect world, we find ourselves being asked, "What's your name again?" And told, "Sorry, there isn't room for you." Or, "I forgot you were here!"

Words like that can be crushing. And that's when dark thoughts creep in. We question whether we are important or not.

Jesus has never forgotten you. You are always on His mind, in His heart—and as Isaiah said, your name is written on His hands. This is a beautiful preface to what happened so many years later as Jesus was nailed to the cross. Those scars never went away, even when He was risen, but Jesus is proud of them. Because they represent you—the one He loved enough to save.

You are never forgotten, alone, or left out by your Savior.

Jesus, thank You for remembering me.

JESUS WEPT

Jesus wept.
JOHN 11:35 NIV

John 11:35 is the shortest verse in the Bible but one of the most impactful verses concerning Jesus' life. When Jesus heard that Lazarus died, we can assume that Jesus knew the end of the story. He knew He was going to raise this man from the dead. But still, when He saw the grief of the sisters who had lost their brother, of the disciples who had lost a friend—when He felt the loss of a spiritual brother Himself—Jesus let Himself cry.

Sometimes this world tells us that we have to hold everything inside. We can't be seen as vulnerable or weak. But the strongest person in the world allowed Himself this simple privilege of crying over a loss. He wants us to feel and to express those feelings.

Our tears never go unnoticed. Jesus mourns with us whenever we grieve. While the pain won't go away quickly, and we don't see an ending in sight, we can find comfort in the moment that Jesus is there with us and understands us. Jesus wept. Find comfort in that today.

Jesus, I'll look for You in times of mourning. I know You understand. Amen.

MUD

*He answered them, "Jesus put mud on
my eyes. I washed and now I see!"*
JOHN 9:15 NLV

You're a counselor at a summer camp with a gigantic mud pit. You schedule a day when anyone who wants to can get muddy. They could get covered head to toe in mud, but there's one rule: they have to clean every bit of it off to get back into your cabin.

In the Bible, there was a guy who was blind, and Jesus spit into the dirt and put mud on the guy's eyes so he could see (John 9:6). Doesn't sound like the beauty treatments you get at a spa, does it? But after the guy cleaned off all the mud from his eyes, he was rewarded.

Jesus' ways of healing aren't always the easiest. Sometimes they're the downright messiest, and we're asked to do a little work and get a little dirty before we can get a little clean. But in the end, when we're finally clear of sin, from pain, we'll know it was all worth it.

---

*Jesus, where is the mud in my life? I want
to do the work to clean it up!*

TURNING THE OTHER CHEEK

Be completely humble and gentle: be patient,
bearing with one another in love.
EPHESIANS 4:2 NIV

That's it. You're done! She shouldn't have posted that, and now she's going on blast. You're in the right, and everyone's gonna know. Your phone's in your hand, and you already have the first couple of words typed out. But you find yourself stopping.

You know you can't. You can't because you know Jesus wouldn't. He said in Matthew 5:39 (NIV), "If anyone slaps you on the right cheek, turn to them the other cheek also." Now this was an extreme example. Jesus would never want you to stay in an abusive situation. But He was telling His followers that the old way of repaying pain with more pain wouldn't actually help anyone.

With Jesus, we can approach those who've hurt us with love instead of revenge. Maybe in time we can forgive them. This process takes humbleness, gentleness, and a whole lot of patience. Thankfully, we're good friends with someone who's perfect at that. Lean on Him when you have to deal with someone who has hurt you.

Jesus, how do I deal with this person who's hurt me?

IN OUR HEARTS

*He has sent the Spirit of His Son into our
hearts. The Spirit cries, "Father!"*
GALATIANS 4:6 NLV

When Jesus returned to heaven, He wasn't leaving us alone. So He left a part of Himself behind. We call this part of Him the Holy Spirit.

John 15:26 (NLV) says, "The Helper (Holy Spirit) will tell about Me when He comes. I will send Him to you from the Father. He is the Spirit of Truth and comes from the Father." This is how Jesus lives on in our hearts. By the Spirit. And this Spirit always tells the truth. He not only shows you what is right and wrong but expresses to you how much you're loved by Jesus. Those things you sometimes tell yourself, like *I'll never be cool enough to hang out with them* or *I'm not worthy of love*, are lies. And the Spirit is there to replace them with truth.

You're absolutely accepted, worthy, and already loved. Find those truths with Jesus in your heart.

Jesus, thanks for being in my heart and not leaving me alone.

SHARING HIM

*Jesus did many other powerful works in front
of His followers. They are not written in this
book. But these are written so you may believe
that Jesus is the Christ, the Son of God.*

JOHN 20:30–31 NLV

Wouldn't you love to know *all* the amazing works Jesus performed
here on earth? We get glimpses of several miracles, but there were
so many more! We don't know for sure how the writers of the
Gospels chose what to put in their writings, but we do know that
they were all trying to do the same thing. Sharing their experiences
so that others could learn about Jesus, and maybe choose to pursue
a relationship with Him. And if we trust Him, we'll find life. That's
what we're asked to do today too.

Take a minute to really think about what Jesus has done in
your life. Think about His miracles and His blessings, any moments
where He has come through for you. Sharing these moments with
others could lead to them taking a chance on Jesus.

---

*Jesus, thank You for all the moments of You in
my life. How do I share that with others?*

SHARING YOURSELF

Zaccheus stood up and said to the Lord, "Lord, see!
Half of what I own I will give to poor people."
LUKE 19:8 NLV

There was a video that went viral about a man going through a busy mall food court asking people to share their food with him. A majority of the people said no. Then the man went and bought food for several homeless men in the area. When he gave the men the food, he also asked each man to share the food with him. Every single homeless man said yes.

Sometimes when we're blessed with things either from this world or from God, we forget what it feels like to be in need and what it feels like to be cared for. So we neglect caring for others. Zaccheus was a very rich man in the Bible, but he didn't know how to care for others. Jesus changed that by changing him as a person.

We too are changed by Jesus, so we should never forget what it's like to share and give to others like He did.

Jesus, what can I share with others in need today?

GIVE WHAT YOU CAN

She put in two very small pieces of money. He said, "I tell you the truth, this poor woman has put in more than all of them."
LUKE 21:2–3 NLV

An old woman gave everything she had to the church she loved. Others in her church—several rich men—gave way more to the offering than she did, but Jesus proclaimed that this woman gave the most. Because she gave all she could. And Jesus knew she would be rewarded for that.

There will be some moments in life when Jesus will ask for time out of your busy schedule, money from your allowance, or talent that you feel you don't have yet. You may feel like you don't have much to give Him, so why give it at all? Remember the story with the fish and loaves? Jesus can do a lot with the little we give Him when we hand it over with complete trust and confidence in Him.

What is Jesus asking of you today? Have you been afraid to give it over to Him?

Jesus, I trust You. I want to. What can I give You?

ON FORGIVING

"Lord, how many times shall I forgive my brother or sister who sins against me? Up to seven times?" Jesus answered, "I tell you, not seven times, but seventy-seven times."
MATTHEW 18:21–22 NIV

You let your friend borrow an important necklace of yours for her date. Then she loses it! She's really sorry, and she's your good friend, so you forgive her. The next day, your friend learns her cousin destroyed her new book by spilling pink drink all over it. She claims she'll never forgive her cousin and never speak to her again!

Encourage your friend to forgive her cousin. Jesus tells a very similar story in Matthew 18. A king forgives the debt of a servant, who then won't forgive someone's debt against him. The king is rightly upset with his servant.

Jesus wants us to forgive others as He's forgiven us. As much as we can. We've been given grace that He wants us to share with others. Even if it's hard. He'll help you.

Jesus, help me to be more willing to forgive others.

THE STORY OF THE RUNAWAY SON

"He was lost and now he is found."
LUKE 15:32 NLV

Did you ever think of running away from home? Maybe when you were little and had a tantrum, you wanted to pack a sandwich and hike to Grandma's house. You knew you would have more fun there!

Jesus told the story of a son who did run away from home. His father had given him an inheritance, and he blew all his money on a lot of stuff that wasn't good for him. In the end, he didn't even have enough money for food. So he returned home, happy to be even a servant for his father. But his father welcomed him back as a beloved child.

Jesus views us the same way. There may be a time when we start to make really bad choices that keep us away from Him, but we'll always be welcomed back with love—an overwhelming amount of love. If you are on the outskirts even now, come back. Jesus is ready to welcome you home.

Jesus, thank You for reminding me that I can always come back to You.

YOU CAN TRUST HIM

*God did not keep His own Son for Himself
but gave Him for us all. Then with His
Son, will He not give us all things?*
ROMANS 8:32 NLV

We all have things we want for our future. You could probably make a list of things you want *right now*. God created us to want things because He gave us special passions and desires. But sometimes these things we want become our everything. They consume our thoughts and our time day after day. We set ourselves up for disappointment when our wants aren't achieved or they don't fulfill us like we thought they would.

Jesus is the proof that God has already given us all we need, so why do we worry over whether God will come through for us? He will hold nothing back! We may not get exactly what we want, but we'll always be given what we need. All we have to do is remain patient and faithful in the highs and the lows of our life, in the disappointments and triumphs. You can trust Him.

---

*Jesus, thank You for being the proof that God
will always provide what we truly need.*

NOT A PAYCHECK

*"But he answered one of them, 'I am not being
unfair to you, friend. Didn't you agree to work
for a denarius? . . . I want to give the one who was
hired last the same as I gave you. Don't I have
the right to do what I want with my own money?
Or are you envious because I am generous?'"*
MATTHEW 20:13–15 NIV

You work at the local ice cream parlor, and the owner tells you
that you'll get paid $100 for the whole day. So you scoop sundaes
until you have one hour left of work. A friend comes by and starts
scooping too. At the end of the day, you're given $100 and your friend
gets $100 too. Doesn't seem fair, does it? You did way more work!

See, Jesus' grace cannot be compared to a paycheck. Because
it has nothing to do with our work. Jesus is generous and doesn't
give His love to only certain folks. He wants everyone to get a
chance to know Him, no matter what time in life they find Him.

---

*Jesus, help me to be happy when others find You. Everyone
deserves the opportunity to have You in their life. Amen.*

164

AS DEEP AND AS WIDE. . .

With both feet planted firmly on love, you'll be able
to take in with all followers of Jesus the extravagant
dimensions of Christ's love. Reach out and experience
the breadth! Test its length! Plumb the depths! Rise to
the heights! Live full lives, full in the fullness of God.
EPHESIANS 3:17–19 MSG

Love is all around us. In the elderly couple still sharing the same booth at the local diner fifty years into their marriage. . . In the shouts of the father cheering encouragement for his daughter as she hits her first home run. . . In the tears of a confession shared with a trusted friend. There is a reason why so many stories focus on the strength of love. It's powerful, and it changes things.

Jesus' love is even more than all these. It's immeasurable. We may never be able to fully understand it. But like love on earth, we don't have to understand it to let it affect us. Just let yourself feel the love. Bask in His love for you. And then share it with everyone around you.

Jesus, You love me. I love You. Thank You!

LEARNING AND TEACHING

Jesus said to them, "What I teach is not
Mine. It is from God Who sent Me."
JOHN 7:16 NLV

We rarely start off knowing exactly how to do something. Driving, cooking, art, a language, singing, you name it—you usually gotta learn from someone else to keep on growing in your own way. You study in school, search online, and borrow books from the library. You may even find a teacher in the subject or craft, and you take classes from them. And if you want, when you're ready, you start teaching others about what you really love.

Jesus wanted His followers to know that He was always teaching what God had taught Him—God, His Father, who sent Him to take care of the world, to save the world. We have to trust that what Jesus said really did come from God and that God believes what Jesus believes. And once we learn more and more about Jesus, growing in our own faith, we may even get to teach others what He's done for us in our lives.

Jesus, I want to learn more about You so
I can share You with others.

HE WILL GIVE LIFE

He will give life.
ROMANS 8:11 NLV

Life is what Jesus wants to offer you. Life that brings about miracles. Life that heals those in pain and soothes those in torment. Life that satisfies hunger and thirst. Life that speaks truth. Life that builds a home. Life that calls you out of the comfortable and into the unknown. Life that walks on water and pulls you from your own roaring ocean. Life that is unafraid to face that ocean. Life that lights up the dark and leads you through the night. Life that never gives up. Life that pushes forward. Life that welcomes you in. Life that gives you new mercies each morning. Life that casts out demons. Life that endures. Life that brings peace. Life that shouts joy. Life that forgives. Life that loves. Life that brings you back from the dead.

Jesus is waiting to offer life—a wonderful, awe-inspiring life—that was always meant for you. And He will never keep it from you. You never have to work yourself ragged to earn it. It is freely given. All you have to do is say yes.

Yes, Jesus. I want this life.

THE WOMAN AT THE WELL

*Jesus said to her, "I am the Christ,
the One talking with you!"*
JOHN 4:26 NLV

This conversation in John 4 seems like any other conversation Jesus had with a stranger. But because of historical context, this conversation was a pretty big deal. First off, this was a woman, and Jesus was speaking openly with her as an equal. Not many men spoke to women in this way. Next, she was a Samaritan, a race that Jews didn't get along with. And finally, she was a social outcast. Gathering water was usually done in groups in the morning. This woman was alone during the day.

Jesus shows us in this interaction that His love is for all. Everyone—no matter gender, race, or social standing—is welcome to have a relationship with the Lord. It shows us that Jesus still welcomes us no matter what we've done in our pasts. And it proves how important testimony is—as hers helped bring a lot of people to Jesus.

Jesus, thank You for the reminder that Your love is for everyone!

YOU FIRST!

"Do not judge, or you too will be judged. . . . First take the plank out of your own eye, and then you will see clearly to remove the speck from your brother's eye."
MATTHEW 7:1, 5 NIV

That boy in your algebra class got detention—again. You've never gotten detention. In fact, you've never even gotten a warning in class. You're the perfect student. Way better than him. Maybe those rumors about him were right. He's just a—whoa! Stop right there!

Jesus never wants us thinking this way about another person. He tells His followers that we're to look at what we've done wrong before we point out the wrongs of someone else. You may be a perfect student, but you realize that maybe you haven't been the nicest big sister. We've all got stuff to work on.

We should know right from wrong, but we should never go around judging others and constantly pointing out their flaws and weaknesses. And we should never ever assume that we're 100 percent perfect all the time and everyone else is evil.

Jesus, whenever I'm judging someone, please stop me. I know we are all in need of Your grace.

SAFE

"If you work these words into your life, you are like a smart carpenter who built his house on solid rock. Rain poured down, the river flooded, a tornado hit—but nothing moved that house. It was fixed to the rock."

MATTHEW 7:24–25 MSG

It was supposed to be a fun evening at the local pool with your friends. But instead, everyone is huddled underneath the snack shack's little roof, waiting out the pelting rain as thunder bellows. The walls shake, but you know they won't fall. It's raining hard now, but soon it will stop and the sun will shine.

Jesus wants us to put our faith in Him like we put our faith in a snack shack to keep us safe from storms. Isn't Jesus so much stronger than that? When we listen to Him and act out what He tells us is best, it's like building a strong house on solid rock. We won't be moved or shaken by life's storms. Instead we endure them, coming out even stronger on the other side.

Jesus, I trust You to keep me safe during storms.

HE WAS ALWAYS THERE

Then beginning with Moses and all the
Prophets, he interpreted for them the things
concerning himself in all the Scriptures.
LUKE 24:27 CSB

Two disciples were walking on a road to Emmaus, talking about something unbelievable. . .Jesus' body was gone! A stranger walked up beside them and asked what had happened. So they told him. And the stranger said that the Messiah's plan of death had to happen so the world could be saved—and that this plan had been in motion for a long time. He even described the times when Jesus was present in the older scriptures. Jesus later revealed Himself to be this stranger.

Jesus was and is always there. He's present in the Old Testament as a promise coming. He is working in the New Testament and today, actively on the page and in our lives. As the two men were blinded to who Jesus really was, we can sometimes be blinded to the moments He meets us in life. Jesus would never leave you. He is still working all things for the best.

Jesus, I want to see You. Reveal Yourself on Your walk with me.

LET'S READ IT AGAIN

"For God loved the world in this way: He gave his one and only Son, so that everyone who believes in him will not perish but have eternal life."
JOHN 3:16 CSB

You've probably seen this verse everywhere—on church signs, on coffee mugs, on bumper stickers... It's one of the most well-known verses of the Bible. So have you ever really stopped to think about what it means when you read it? You may have gotten so used to it you don't even really think about it!

Let's take a minute today to read this verse one more time. Think about what it really means to you. God loved the world so much that He gave up His Son—something very valuable to Him—so that everyone would be able to get the chance to spend eternity with Him. In perfect peace. In wonderful abundance. Away from darkness and pain.

We should hope to never get tired of reading such truth. That we are loved and saved by Jesus!

I don't ever want to gloss over this verse again, Jesus. I want to really think about what it means.

PRESS Restart

*In the beginning was the Word, and the Word
was with God, and the Word was God.*
JOHN 1:1 CSB

Genesis 1:1 (CSB) says, "In the beginning God created the heavens and the earth." And amazingly, Jesus was there. Jesus was with God, and He is God. So He knew what the world was supposed to be like, how we were all supposed to live as His beloved creation. So Jesus knew what He was doing when He pressed RESTART, giving everyone a second chance to have a relationship with His Father. He gave His life to restart our relationship with God.

In John 1:1, it says that Jesus was the Word—a living, breathing testimony of God's promises and His love for us. Jesus wasn't here just to deliver a letter from God as so many thought. Jesus was the letter. A letter of love and hope in a time of grief and barrenness. So we have the chance to hit RESTART and begin a new life in Him.

Living Word, I want to receive and share the message of You today.

CARE FOR OTHERS PART ONE

"For the Son of Man did not come to be cared
for. He came to care for others. He came to
give His life so that many could be bought by
His blood and be made free from sin."

MARK 10:45 NLV

Your friend's life is perfect. Her posts online are stunning. She gets the best grade in school and the lead in the musical. You love her, but you're also a little jealous of her.

Then she calls you crying. Her life isn't as perfect as you had thought.

It'd be so easy to tell her that her life is great and she has no reason to be sad. But caring for others the right way, the way they need, is rarely easy. Jesus knew this well. But He never once let how He was feeling get in the way of truly loving someone else. So when you get that call, the world may tell you to tell her to suck it up, but Jesus will be there to remind you that everyone needs care sometimes.

Jesus, it's hard, but I want to help someone
even when I don't want to.

CARE FOR OTHERS PART TWO

"For the Son of Man came not to be cared for. He came to care for others. He came to give His life so that many could be bought by His blood and made free from the punishment of sin."

<small>MATTHEW 20:28 NLV</small>

This looks like the same verse as before. But it's from a different Gospel! Matthew heard Jesus say this too and thought it was important. Jesus said this right after two brothers fought about who would sit at His right hand in heaven. But then Jesus tells them that they shouldn't do good works just to be rewarded. We should do them because we truly love Jesus and love others.

Jesus came and cared for others with no expectation of reward. He only wanted to share the truth that He will free those He loves from the punishment of sin. When we care for others, we shouldn't do it so they'll help us later on or we'll get a gift card in the mail! We should help others because we want to.

Jesus, I want to help others even when I don't feel like it because I know that's what You'd do.

LOST CAUSE

*"Today salvation has come to this house, because
this man, too, is a son of Abraham. For the Son
of Man came to seek and to save the lost."*
LUKE 19:9–10 NIV

A lost cause. That's something you don't think will ever get better or get fixed. Maybe you have someone in your life you view as a lost cause. They never seem to make the right choice. You don't know what to do. Or maybe that person is you. So you *really* don't know what to do. Either way, there's good news.

Jesus loves a lost cause. He came to save a world that looked a whole lot like a lost cause, covered in sin and separated from God. He came to not only find the world lost in its darkness but save it. Salvation has come.

Find comfort that no one is too lost from Jesus' rescue. No one is too far gone. He is there, working and present in your life. Waiting for you to grasp on to Him.

---

*Jesus, lost causes are why You came. I want to remember
that when I'm dealing with one in my own life. You can fix it.*

GRACE AND TRUTH ARE GIFTS

Out of his fullness we have all received
grace in the place of grace already given.
For the law was given through Moses; grace
and truth came through Jesus Christ.
JOHN 1:16–17 NIV

Imagine getting everything you want. It looks good, right? That career, that marriage, that accomplishment, that dream life! But still something is missing. All these things—though wonderful blessings—still don't have the power to make your life complete.

Grace is powerful. Truth is powerful. Jesus is powerful. And He is the gift that you never thought you needed, given to us on top of our everyday blessings. Because of His fullness, His over-the-top unmatchable goodness, we benefit as this powerful grace and truth wash over us. He gives us this grace and truth over and over again, throughout our entire lives.

You may be wondering how those are gifts. Well, grace is what gives us the chance at eternity with Jesus, and truth helps us live the closest life we can to eternity in our earthly bodies. It is really all we need.

Jesus, thank You for all the gifts You give me. Amen!

JESUS' POWER

The conquering power that brings the world
to its knees is our faith. The person who wins
out over the world's ways is simply the one
who believes Jesus is the Son of God.
1 John 5:4–5 MSG

Jesus' power is walking on water. Jesus' power is calming storms. Jesus' power is feeding the five thousand. Jesus' power is healing the sick. It is standing up for what's right even when He was the only one standing. It is disregarding what others thought of Him. It is taking on a punishment for the sake of someone else.

Jesus' power is dying on the cross. Jesus' power is forsaking that cross by defeating death three days later.

And that power lives inside you. You've got the power to stand up, to stand out, to help others, to be courageous in life, simply because you've got faith in Jesus. Just by knowing Him, you've already overcome anything that life throws your way.

Jesus, I'm powerful too because of You. Thank You!

MORE THAN THIS

*But there's far more to life for us. We're citizens
of high heaven! We're waiting the arrival
of the Savior, the Master, Jesus Christ.*
PHILIPPIANS 3:20 MSG

Sleep, eat, school, practice, work, eat, sleep. That's what your life has been the last few months. At first, everything was exciting. School meant new classes. Practice meant getting to do what you love. But in between essays and workouts and dinners, things started getting. . .boring. You started thinking, *There's gotta be more than this.*

There is. We may feel like we're missing out on something during the mundane days of life because we know that as followers of Christ we were meant for a different place. But that doesn't mean we can't find contentment and joy in this period of waiting right now.

Jesus wants us to share in the peace that we have an eternal home, but we're here right now for a very special reason. So in the waiting, find ways to enjoy that reason. He wants you to.

---

*Jesus, when life starts getting boring, remind me
that I'm here for a reason. I want to enjoy it.*

THE WOMAN AND THE PERFUME

*Jesus said to the woman, "Your faith
has saved you; go in peace."*
LUKE 7:50 NIV

Can you imagine this odd scene? You're sitting at a table, eating with Jesus, when a stranger comes in and pours perfume on Jesus' feet. Then she cleans His feet with her hair and her tears. Very awkward.

But Jesus didn't think so. He even said that this woman would be remembered greatly after He was gone and the gospel is shared (Mark 14:6–9). And spoiler alert: she is! When the world looks at our desperate pleas for forgiveness and help as weakness, Jesus admires it greatly. Because it shows that we've chosen to put all things aside—what others think of us, our pride, our egos—to focus clearly on what Jesus can do for us.

Are you letting yourself get in the way of laying everything down in front of Jesus? What are some things you need to set aside to let Him meet you where you're at?

---

*Jesus, I'm sometimes afraid and ashamed to say I'm
in desperate need of You. But I do need You today.*

CHEER THEM ON!

Our bodies are made up of many parts. None of these parts have the same use. There are many people who belong to Christ. And yet, we are one body which is Christ's. We are all different but we depend on each other.
ROMANS 12:4–5 NLV

A softball team can't be made out of only pitchers. A choir wouldn't sound as amazing with only sky-high sopranos. Even our bodies are made up of different parts that do different things that all work together to keep us going. We can't all be the same.

In the body of Christ, the large group of people that are His followers, we're all different. But we all come together for the same purpose. To love others in the name of Jesus. Everyone does that differently most of the time! Jesus wants us to be different but also to depend on one another. Be content and joyful with what you're adding to the kingdom, and cheer on your siblings in Christ as they share His love in the way they do best. You're all making the world a better place!

Jesus, help me to cheer others on as we all share You. Amen!

DON'T BE DIVIDED

"Every kingdom divided against itself is headed for destruction, and a house divided against itself falls."
LUKE 11:17 CSB

You want to focus on the battles of the Civil War fought in your town for your history project. But the guy you're paired up with wants to work on the first-known football team in your state. Instead of coming to a compromise, you both work on your own idea, so by the time the project's deadline comes, neither of you are ready. If you had worked together, you might have gotten the idea of how both the histories of American football and Civil War battles come together in a famous historical novel.

Jesus knew that His followers' best chance at spreading His message would be by working together. Working together usually leads to great success. But if a group is divided, there is no chance they'll succeed. If we're too busy fighting with other Christ followers about little things, we miss out on showing the world the big picture of Jesus—He loves the world and came to save it!

Jesus, I'm done with fighting others. I want to focus on what really matters—You!

PROSPER

"So my word that comes from my mouth will not return to me empty, but it will accomplish what I please and will prosper in what I send it to do."

Isaiah 55:11 csb

It looks like gray rain for days, but when those beautiful flowers take over, you know there was a purpose for it all. You probably remember how Jesus is the Living Word (John 1:1). God says that just as rain won't leave the earth without helping flowers grow, His Word won't leave this world without changing it.

And change it He did. He saved the world. And not only did He make a way for us to survive this world but He left us with a way to enjoy this life, to truly live in abundance, in joy, in peace. Jesus' life happened so that we could prosper. So that we could grow in Him during our time on earth to become who we all were truly meant to be. Because of Him we can do more than just wake up each day. We can really have an abundant life!

Jesus, I would love to do more than survive. I want to prosper.

USED TO IT

His disciples did not understand these things at first. However, when Jesus was glorified, then they remembered that these things had been written about him and that they had done these things to him.

JOHN 12:16 CSB

We're amazed by falling stars because we don't see them very often. It's a special experience to see one flashing across the sky. But if we saw one or two daily, a falling star would lose its specialness. It would just be a part of our lives; we'd be used to it.

The disciples were sometimes so used to life with Jesus that they didn't realize what was happening. It was just normal life! It wasn't until Jesus died and rose again and then returned to heaven that they realized that what had been written about Jesus had actually come to pass. And they were a part of it!

Thankfully, we're given the chance to see the whole story up front. We can believe right away that what Jesus did and said is true. We never have to get used to it.

Jesus, I don't ever want to get used to the amazing story of Your life and death.

GOD-EXPRESSION

No one has ever seen God, not so much as a glimpse.
This one-of-a-kind God-Expression, who exists at the
very heart of the Father, has made him plain as day.

JOHN 1:18 MSG

Expressionist art is all about the artist portraying emotion rather than an exact representation of the real world. Pieces of art that fall into this category were created to invoke emotions and feelings. In this verse, Jesus is referred to as "this one-of-a-kind God-Expression."

Nothing and no one is like Jesus. He is God in human form, an expression of divinity. And as an expression, Jesus was created to invoke a strong emotional reaction. He was always meant to move the hearts of His creation and to pull us back to Him.

So when you feel a strong reaction when it comes to Jesus— embrace it! Ask Him to help you understand it. If you haven't yet felt a strong feeling toward Him, don't feel bad. It may be that He is waiting for the right time to reach out and move your heart.

Jesus, You truly are an expression of
God. Of who He wants us to be.

WORSHIP HIM

He answered, "I tell you, if they were to
keep silent, the stones would cry out."
LUKE 19:40 CSB

As wonderful and amazing as Jesus is, He doesn't need us to worship Him. He actually claims that even if His people don't worship Him, then the rocks will cry out in praise. And doesn't nature already do so, just by being? Waterfalls, large rocks, canyons, the sea, mountains—all of them glorify His name just by existing.

We are meant to do the same. And this doesn't mean just worshipping Him on Sundays. As His most beloved creation, we have the chance to worship Him by being ourselves every single day. By loving others. By working hard at our calling. By spending time with Him and allowing Him into our lives.

Jesus doesn't need you to worship Him, but He wants you to. He wants you to want Him in your life as much as He desires you in His. Praise Him today!

Jesus, how can I worship You more each day?

NO WORRIES

*"Therefore do not worry about tomorrow,
for tomorrow will worry about itself. Each
day has enough trouble of its own."*

MATTHEW 6:34 NIV

You're at your best friend's sleepover, but as everyone is having fun watching movies and laughing, your mind is somewhere else entirely. All you can think about is everything you have to do next week. You're missing out on some great experiences with your friends.

So you worry a lot about what will happen. You worry about your family and friends. You worry about tomorrow, next week, next year. Jesus wants us to care about our futures, but He doesn't want thoughts of tomorrow to keep us up at night or one thing gone wrong to send us into panic mode. He doesn't want us to miss out on today.

Jesus asks us to cast our anxieties on Him. Don't let them take away your strength or your joy. And don't let them take you away from all the goodness that can be found in this present moment. When you feel nervous, give it to Jesus. He wants it.

*Jesus, I want to enjoy my today. I give You
all my worries about tomorrow.*

NO MATTER WHAT

Jesus said to him, "Friend, do what you came to do."
MATTHEW 26:50 NLV

There is nothing you can do that will ever take you away from the love of Jesus. Let that sink in. You are His beloved, His everything. His love for you knows no bounds. No matter what you do, what you feel, you are fully known and loved by Jesus.

Judas was Jesus' friend. He lived many days by His side. Jesus considered him like a brother. And Judas still betrayed Him. And yet, when Judas approached Jesus on that fateful night, Jesus did not get angry. He did not condemn. Instead, He called Judas what He was to the Son of God: "Friend."

That's how much Jesus loves Judas. And that's how much Jesus loves you. Nothing will ever get in the way of Him having a relationship and a friendship with you. His love will chase after you, no matter how far you've gone.

Trust His love. Trust Him.

Jesus, I'll trust that no matter what, You will always love me. Thank You. I love You too.

SCRIPTURE INDEX

ABOUT THE AUTHOR

Ellie Zumbach is a freelance writer and actor in northeastern Ohio. She earned a BA in Creative Writing from Malone University. Other Barbour books by her include *180 Prayers for a Woman of Confidence* and *God Calls You Strong, Girl* (an ECPA bestseller). She has always believed that stories are some of the most important things in the world and spent her years growing up on a small dairy farm reading as many as she could.